GALLIPOLI PHOTOGRAPHED
Images of Gallipoli: Photographs from the collection of Ross J. Bastiaan.
By P.A. Pedersen.

(OUP Australia, £20 ISBN 0 19 554889 2)

Photography as a pastime or, more properly, as a means of recording other pastimes, was well established in Britain by the outbreak of the Great War. Portable and reliable cameras were freely available to those who could afford such things and many families of the middle classes and above owned cameras and growing albums of family snapshots.

The camera had already been to war on a number of occasions before August 1914, but usually in hands of "professional" photographers who could cope with the heavy and unwieldy equipment. The Boer War saw an increase in private photography, daylight loading roll film and folding cameras (especially the Kodak) making the amateur photographer's life much less encumbered.

The ranks of the BEF of 1914 included many more photographers than has generally been realised and it was their activities that soon led to a simple General Routine Order: "The taking of photographs is not permitted", an instruction that, in back areas at least, appears to have been largely ignored throughout the war. In Egypt photography was certainly forbidden in mosques and tombs (on the grounds that it was "particularly offensive to Moslems") but there were few other restrictions, and in Mesopotamia it was positively encouraged (except as regards "executions or floggings").

On the Gallipoli Peninsula photography was certainly restricted, but it went on anyway, after all there was so very little that the enemy could not either see for himself or accurately guess at. However, as Ross Bastiaan points out in a note to this selection from his collection, the vast majority of these images were "little more than snapshots, intended for the photographer's family album" and wholly unlike those in *Images of Gallipoli* that were clearly taken by some with "an eye".

The photographs reproduced in *Images of Gallipoli* were probably taken by Surgeon C.H.S. Taylor, RNVR, commander of the 3rd Field Ambulance of the Royal Naval Division but, despite having had access to Surgeon Taylor's service record ("sketched rather well"), Dr. P.A. Pederson tells us remarkably little about the supposed photographer in his otherwise straightforward text and captions. However, the qualities of the photographs far outweigh any possible shortcomings in the text and here we have to be grateful for the photographer's eye, the nature of the original film and camera and the quality of reproduction achieved by the Australian printers.

Images of Gallipoli presents an unrivalled, coherent pictorial narrative of the war on the Peninsula, as well as fascinating glimpses of the war at sea and in the air around and above the Dardanelles. Of particular interest to this reviewer are the photographs of the RND's trench weapons (including Leach/Gammage catapults), of HMS *Ark Royal* and her complement of seaplanes, and of the dummy HMS *Tiger*.

Highly recommended.

Peter T. Scott

IMAGES OF GALLIPOLI

Also by P.A. Pedersen

Monash as Military Commander
(Melbourne University Press, 1985)

IMAGES OF GALLIPOLI

Photographs from the collection of Ross J. Bastiaan

P. A. Pedersen

OXFORD
UNIVERSITY PRESS

Melbourne
Oxford   Auckland   New York

OXFORD UNIVERSITY PRESS AUSTRALIA

Oxford New York Toronto
Delhi Bombay Calcutta Madras Karachi
Petaling Jaya Singapore Hong Kong Tokyo
Nairobi Dar es Salaam Cape Town
Melbourne Auckland
and associated companies in
Berlin Ibadan

OXFORD is a trade mark of Oxford University Press

National Library of Australia
Cataloguing-in-Publication data:

Pedersen, P.A. (Peter Andreas), 1952–
    Images of Gallipoli: photographs from
    the collection of Ross J. Bastiaan.

    Bibliography.
    ISBN 0 19 554889 2.

    1. Bastiaan, Ross J. — Photograph collections.
    2. World War, 1914–1918 — Campaigns — Turkey
    — Gallipoli Peninsula. 3. World War, 1914–1918
    — Campaigns — Turkey — Gallipoli Peninsula —
    Photography. 4. War photography — Turkey —
    Gallipoli Peninsula. I. Title.

940.4′25′0222

Edited by Chris Nicol
Designed by Ron Hampton
Typeset by Abb-typesetting Pty Ltd, Victoria
Printed by Impact Printing, Melbourne
Published by Oxford University Press,
253 Normanby Road, South Melbourne, Australia

Publisher's note: Some photographs in the book have been
cropped to remove flaws or to allow larger reproduction
of detail.

Contents

Surgeon C.H.S. Taylor outside his dugout on Officers' Walk above X Beach, towards the end of the Gallipoli campaign. His gaunt face, sunken eyes and pensive expression bear eloquent testimony to the strain of almost eight months of continuous active service in the Dardanelles. This picture should be compared with the shot of Taylor on p. 75 taken a few months earlier.

Introduction

The photographs in this book convey much of the unique flavour of the Gallipoli campaign. They were probably taken by a British officer, Surgeon Charles Henry Shinglewood Taylor, a member of the Royal Naval Volunteer Reserve and 32 years old in 1915. He was mentioned in despatches for his 'distinguished and gallant conduct' while commanding the 3rd Field Ambulance of the Royal Naval Division (RND) on the Gallipoli Peninsula. According to his service record, Taylor 'sketched rather well' and his artist's eye is evident in many of his photographs.[1] Taylor's standing as a commanding officer may also have helped because security regulations were tightened in 1915 to discourage the private use of cameras and the keeping of diaries. But diaries could be maintained discreetly and they satisfied a basic human need by allowing an individual constrained by a highly disciplined environment to articulate thoughts which the censor would otherwise suppress. Photography was harder to hide, which partly explains the dearth of good photographs taken during the campaign. So we are very much in Taylor's debt.

Taylor was not a fighting soldier, but the morale of fighting soldiers depended very much on whether units like his functioned efficiently. Soldiers fight better when they are confident in the knowledge that they will receive prompt and skilled medical attention if they are wounded or sick. But the ability of a field ambulance to dispense such treatment in 1915 stemmed largely from the initiative its commander showed in overcoming the problems inherent in any new and unproven concept. The first field ambulance was formed in March 1906 as a result of faults in the casualty evacuation system demonstrated during the Boer War. The inability of its horse-drawn transport to evacuate casualties quickly enough, and other teething problems, did not become apparent until after the First World War began. Under Taylor the 3rd Field Ambulance would probably have comprised eleven officers, nine of them doctors, and 172 other ranks. Its bearer division could collect, and its tent division could treat and temporarily hold, up to 150 wounded.

According to the medical doctrine of the time, Taylor's duties would have included siting the advanced dressing station, which his ambulance would set up about 2000 metres behind the front line and to which the stretcher bearers took the wounded. Such proximity to the front made this the most dangerous and, therefore, the most arduous stage of the evacuation, both for the bearer and for the casualty. Taylor would have had to plan and execute alternative measures if enemy action disrupted the process. The operation of walking-wounded collection posts, designed to keep less seriously wounded away from the advanced dressing station, might also have been his responsibility. From the advanced dressing station, motor transport would transfer patients to a main dressing station up to 7000 metres further back, which could hold some 500 casualties. If the 3rd Field Ambulance had established the advanced dressing station and was handling bearer duties, another field ambulance would set up the main dressing station. The third of the RND's three field ambulances would be held in reserve.[2]

The concept of a naval division was even newer than that of the field ambulance. Plans had long existed for the formation of a Royal Marine Brigade to assist the fleet by carrying out sea-borne landings in time of war. The brigade reinforced Ostend at the end of August 1914 against a German attack (which, in the event, did not materialize). At the same time, large numbers of naval reservists, who were surplus to fleet requirements, were formed into two naval brigades at the instigation of the First Lord of the Admiralty, Winston Churchill. They joined the Marine Brigade, the three brigades constituting the RND. The men called themselves 'Churchill's Pets' when things went well and 'Churchill's Innocent Victims' when they didn't.[3] They called themselves victims at Antwerp where the RND's half-trained troops lost heavily in the hastily mounted and unsuccessful attempt to deny the city to the Germans in October. The RND's three field ambulances were formed as part of the rebuilding of the division after Antwerp.

Troops from the RND feature prominently in Taylor's photographs. Douglas Jerrold, the RND's historian, lavished the same praise upon them as one would find given to troops in any one of a dozen other divisional histories.[4] But the RND was different and the men knew it. There was never more than one naval division and it retained its naval ranks and customs throughout the war. Taylor is often seen wearing the division's khaki cap of the naval type and with a naval curl on his sleeves instead of the star or crown which showed the rank of a military officer. Possibly because it was unique, the RND attracted 'some of the leading intellectuals and other brilliant young men of the day'.[5] Rupert Brooke, the poet, Denys Browne, the musician, Patrick Shaw-Stewart, an outstanding Oxford Scholar, Arthur Asquith, talented son of the Prime Minister, and Bernard Freyberg, destined to win the Victoria Cross and become Governor-General of New Zealand, all numbered among its junior officers. The artist Taylor, fluent in French and Dutch, probably felt at home with them.

Still short of three battalions and with no artillery, the RND began embarking for the Dardanelles in early February 1915. The Allies were hoping to seize Constantinople, thereby knocking Turkey out of the war and opening up communications to beleaguered Russia. For Churchill and others of the 'Eastern school' who saw the Triple Alliance (Germany, Austria-Hungary and Turkey) as a single entity, the plan corresponded to an attack on the German strategic flank. If successful, it would force Germany to divert resources from the decisive theatre in France and so weaken the German grip on the deadlocked Western Front. It would also enable Britain to exploit her principal advantage of sea power, which had hitherto been neglected.[6]

Yet the concept was couched in a vagueness and ambiguity which would ultimately epitomize the campaign itself. How, precisely, asks John North, was 'a naval force, unsupported by a land force . . . to "take" a precipitous tract of country and a city of a million inhabitants?'[7] And while capturing Constantinople would have been an important success and might have rallied the wavering Balkan states to the Allied cause as the Easterners hoped, 'this would not have solved the basic problem of defeating Germany'.[8] Unlike her opponents, Germany had the advantage of interior lines, which allowed her to transfer troops quickly between fronts, and unity of command. Moreover, supplying Russia with war material was not a practical proposition in 1915. The Western Allies were themselves strapped for munitions—by March, British artillery on the Western Front was limited to three rounds daily per gun.[9]

Nevertheless, Churchill's enthusiasm led to the despatch of an Anglo-French fleet of mainly obsolete ships to force the Dardanelles by bombarding and destroying the Turkish forts on both shores of the waterway. The attack began desultorily on 19 February but within three weeks the fleet was stopped short of the Narrows, about one mile across and the chokepoint of the forty-mile-long ribbon of water leading to the Sea of Marmara and Constantinople. Taylor's superbly detailed picture of a 9.4 inch gun (p. 53), wrecked in its emplacement at Fort No. 1 on the cliffs of Cape Helles, might make this seem surprising. But the shelling of the forts themselves was much less effective. The flat trajectory of the naval guns simply could not achieve the destruction wrought by the plunging fire of howitzers on land.

The use of marines from the ships, and from the RND's Marine Brigade, for demolition work on some of the forts already admitted the principle of providing military assistance to the fleet. Fears that the bombardment might not succeed without the help of a strong military force gradually gained momentum. The RND, the Australian and New Zealand Army Corps and, after great equivocation, the British 29th Division, were earmarked, while the French contributed a division (later a corps). Secretary of State for War

Kitchener described their role as being limited to minor operations such as occupying forts. But on 18 March, three battleships were sunk by mines and three more severely damaged in what would be the navy's last attempt to break through. If the grand design was to proceed, the only option seemed to be 'a deliberate and progressive military operation carried out in force to make good a passage for the Navy'.[10] Major-General E. K. G. Sixsmith sums up:

> The two most tragic elements in the Gallipoli story are the decisions, first to launch the naval attack without military support, and second to call off this naval attack in order to wait for military support. There seems little doubt that if Churchill and the admirals had known that Kitchener would make three divisions or so available, they would have preferred to wait for a prepared combined operation.[11]

The Commander-in-Chief (C-in-C) of the Mediterranean Expeditionary Force (MEF), General Sir Ian Hamilton, was 'an infantryman with all the brilliance and dash usually associated with the cavalry leader'.[12] Three times recommended for the Victoria Cross, he had seen more active service than any other senior serving officer in the British Army. He was 'slight, alert and eager' in appearance and charming in manner.[13] Taylor's photograph (p. 84) captures Hamilton well, typically gripping his scarf with his shattered left hand as he is in the well-known picture of him aboard HMS *Triad*.[14] In Taylor's photograph Hamilton did not know he was in the camera's lens, unlike the photograph on the *Triad*.

Hamilton's plan reflected his intelligence, imagination and optimism. Any hope of strategic surprise had long gone. The Turks had reinforced the two divisions they had had at the Dardanelles in February with four more, thus outnumbering Hamilton's force. Hamilton hoped to offset the disadvantages facing him by using deception and ruses to conceal his principal line of assault, so gaining tactical surprise. Seeking to tie down the main Turkish forces on the first day, the RND would feint at Bulair on the neck of the Peninsula while the French would land briefly on the Asiatic shore, hoping to do the same there. The Australians and New Zealanders were to cross the Peninsula just north of Gaba Tepe, cutting off the Turkish troops in the south where the 29th Division would make the principal landing on five small beaches. The interval between Hamilton's departure from London on 13 March and the first landings on 25 April was forty-three days. The planning of the Normandy invasion took over a year.[15]

The haste told in many ways. The RND embarked before an opposed landing seemed likely and so was loaded as if its destination was a friendly port. Certain troops were in one ship, their transport in another and their horses in a third.[16] The 29th Division found equipment belonging to troops destined for one beach loaded in ships carrying troops to another beach. The Greek island of Lemnos had been selected as a base but its harbour at

Mudros lacked facilities for loading and unloading ships and its exposed waters became too rough for small boats even in a moderate breeze. The RND was subsequently sent to Port Said for transhipment, the remainder of the MEF going to Alexandria for this purpose. Ammunition was in short supply, a deficiency further complicated by the RND's use of a different type of rifle to those in the other Imperial divisions. As it was, the amount of ammunition allotted was barely sufficient for one sustained battle.[17] There were not enough engineers or signallers, no trench stores of any kind and no materials for jetty or pier construction.

Not only were these matters beyond the control of the majority of men but the mood of the times pushed them beyond their conscious concerns as well. During the outward voyage from England, Taylor was struck by the ramparts at Malta (see p. 30) and then busy Port Said, (p. 31) where the division received 'a fine welcome by all the vessels in the harbour, which were of various nationalities'.[18] Cairo duplicated the sights and sounds of Port Said on a larger scale. Its narrow, bustling streets and ancient monuments, particularly the Sphinx, captivated Taylor even more (pp. 32, 33). Taylor also took many photographs of aircraft and ships, including a rare picture (p. 44) of the dummy HMS *Tiger* (itself never at Gallipoli), which 'resembled the proper ship exactly except for having too much free-board'.[19] One superb sequence shows HMS *Ark Royal* winching one of her Short seaplanes aboard (pp. 98–101). The sights at Mudros (p. 34) evoked Masefield's description: 'ships, more ships, perhaps, than any port of modern times has known; they seemed like half the ships of the world'.[20]

Because Mudros was overcrowded, the RND diverted to the island of Skyros on leaving Port Said. Taylor captured the practice landings on Skyros, carried out with drill-like precision (p. 37): 'In perfect formation we reached the rocky beach; we scrambled over the rocks and soon had a continuous line at the foot of the very steep slopes.'[21] The impression created is misleading, as it is with his record of training aboard ship. Though showing great promise, the RND was 'still short of training', remarked the Official Historian.[22] The realization was growing that the landing, the largest combined operation yet attempted, would be difficult. In a message to his 29th Division, which was also read to some units of the RND, Major-General Hunter-Weston warned of 'heavy losses by bullets, by shells, by mines and by drowning . . .'.[23] But the RND, like the rest of the MEF, was swept by 'an extraordinary exhilaration at the prospect of battle'. Rupert Brooke, shortly to die of blood poisoning from an insect bite, had 'not imagined that fate could be so benign . . . I am filled with confident and glorious hopes'.[24] Many men in the RND had bought copies of the *Iliad* and 'wrote rapturously of the romantic possibilities of the campaign'.[25]

Taylor probably shared in this euphoria. But in the last days before the landing, he may well have been worried by events of which few others were aware. The masterly reorganization and re-embarkation of the army in Egypt and the equally meticulous planning of the landing, were done by Hamilton's small General Staff. Their success reinforced his antipathy for a large administrative staff. Newly arrived from England, the administrative staff, including Hamilton's Director of Medical Services, Surgeon-General Birrell, were again left behind, this time in Alexandria, when Hamilton returned to Lemnos on 7 April. When Birrell rejoined General Headquarters (GHQ), he was astounded to find that the General Staff had already prepared a medical plan allowing for not more than 3000 casualties throughout the MEF on the first day of the landing, of whom the two hospital ships allotted could only accommodate 700. Birrell submitted an ill-received memorandum to GHQ which stated that 10 000 was a more realistic casualty figure, and also arranged for three additional hospital ships and seven transports which, together, could receive most of them.[26] But the extra ships did not arrive until after the landings had begun.

The main landing at Cape Helles was at V Beach, where sixty-four Turkish soldiers atop a steep, grassy slope looked down on a strip of sand some 300 yards long and ten wide, enclosed at its eastern and western ends respectively by the mediaeval fort at Sedd-el-Bahr and Fort No. 1 on the cliffs. The Turks waited until the boats had almost reached the shore before opening a withering fire. Whole boatloads were hit and drifted aimlessly. One boat got ashore because its crew took cover behind it, pushing the boat ahead of them as they swam.[27] The fire then switched to the gangways and sally-ports of a ten-year-old collier, the *River Clyde*. A modern Trojan horse, she had been grounded a short distance from the beach and was disgorging her infantry through holes cut in her side. They presented the Turks with 'a target which was not unlike the line of moving objects one sees sometimes in a shooting gallery at a village fair'.[28] The invaders stood no chance. A British aviator who witnessed the slaughter recorded that, for half a mile off shore, the calm sea was a crescent of red.[29] But for the successful French diversion at Kum Kale, the V Beach landing would have been even harder pressed. At W Beach, half a mile to the west of V and the only other landing place covered by barbed wire and machine guns, the attackers also lost heavily before the Turks withdrew. The sea was crimson there as well.

The events at these beaches left an indelible impression, not just on the survivors but on all those who served at Helles, Taylor not least among them. His collection boasts many shots of V Beach (see pp. 56–61), some of them taken from the Turkish trenches, as if Taylor was trying to appreciate what his comrades on the beach faced. The historical analogy, which Liddell Hart later coined so eloquently, may have sprung to his mind: 'Here the invaders ran, like gladiators, into a gently sloping arena designed by nature and arranged by the Turks—themselves ensconced in surrounding seats—for a butchery.'[30] The black-painted *River Clyde* rises ghost-like from the shore (p. 58). One looks at the beach in the picture taken from the collier (p. 59) and shudders. The photographs of W Beach (pp. 68, 69) show a slope appreciably greater than that at V. But they cannot reveal the undertow within feet of the waterline that was an added hazard for the heavily-laden men stumbling towards the shore.

The RND was largely spared this carnage. Although its Anson Battalion contributed detachments to the main landings, the division was principally charged with the feint at Bulair. Taylor's photograph (pp. 46) shows the dawn sun struggling to shine through formless grey clouds as the men aboard their eleven transports watched the slow bombardment of Bulair, which continued through the day. Towards dusk, boats were ostentatiously lowered and headed for the beach, turning back once darkness shrouded their movements. Freyberg then swam ashore and lit flares, hoping to simulate the landing of a large body of troops. After the war, some Turkish officers claimed that the handling of the transports showed that a landing was not intended.[31] But von Sanders, the Turks' German commander on the Peninsula, remained at Bulair all that day and ordered the reinforcement of its two divisions.[32] On 29 April the RND finally went ashore and into support above W Beach. Sniping was intense. Joseph Murray, an RND soldier, noted: 'The firing line was not a continuous line, just a series of outposts strung across the Peninsula.'[33]

Meanwhile the RND's Plymouth Battalion had figured prominently in one of the campaign's seemingly endless 'might have beens'. It was one of two battalions ordered to land at Y beach, about a mile to the west of Krithia. Through this late addition to the original scheme, Hamilton hoped to secure his western flank at Helles and possibly threaten the rear of the Turks defending V and W Beaches. The landing was unopposed and parties penetrated as far as a deserted Krithia and to Gully Ravine (see p. 70–2), a mile to the south. But Hamilton's foresight went unrewarded.

Without news of the main landings and perplexed by the failure of the advance he expected to reach him, the commander at Y dug in above the beach. After eleven undisturbed hours, Turkish counter-attacks began and continued through the night. Private Horace Bruckshaw of the Plymouth Battalion wrote that the fire was 'so hot that one dare not move the little finger'.[34] Anticipating a naval bombardment, the Turks withdrew at dawn on 26 April. Their opponents were retiring as well. Bruckshaw remarked: 'This order we could not understand . . . for we could see absolutely nothing to warrant it.'[35]

By midday the re-embarkation was completed—like the landing, without a shot being fired. The Official Historian called Y Beach perhaps the most disappointing of all the landings:

> In deciding to throw a force ashore at that point Sir Ian Hamilton would seem to have hit upon the key of the whole situation . . . it is as certain as anything can be in war that a bold advance from Y on the morning of the 25th April must have freed the southern beaches that morning, and ensured a decisive victory for the 29th Division.[36]

Hamilton must bear much of the blame for what occurred. Witnessing the disaster on V Beach from HMS *Queen Elizabeth*, the C-in-C had asked Hunter-Weston whether he might like to divert troops to Y, where Hamilton knew that the troops were successfully ashore. Off W Beach and unaware of how the wider battle was developing, Hunter-Weston rejected his suggestion. Obsessed by Helles, Hunter-Weston ignored pleas for reinforcements from Y on 26 April, telling Hamilton he had none to spare. Hamilton sent a French brigade to Y on his own initiative but the evacuation was already underway.

Much the same happened at S Beach on the eastern side of V Beach. The battalion landing there quickly swept aside token resistance but stopped to await the advance from V Beach instead of taking it in rear. V and W Beaches could also have been isolated had more troops gone ashore to the west of W, at X Beach, the other successful landing and from whose clifftops Taylor later took many pictures (see pp. 112–15). As at S and Y, the troops on X remained on the defensive throughout the day. Detailed as it was, Hamilton's plan did not allow for partial success. Powerless to influence the battle directly because he had no general reserve at his disposal, Hamilton was nonetheless reluctant to take over the reins from Hunter-Weston. According to one who watched Hunter-Weston on the bridge of HMS *Euryalus*, the chain of command seemed 'fragile and at times almost impalpable'.[37]

On 29 April the bearer division of the 3rd Field Ambulance landed at W Beach. Exposed to constant rifle and artillery fire, particularly on the beaches where they brought the wounded for evacuation, the stretcher bearers' work was exhausting. The tent division, including Taylor, stayed on board the hospital ship *Somali*. Conditions were grim, for the medical arrangements had collapsed completely. The trouble was that Birrell's hastily revised plan had been predicated on a quick advance inland, thus gaining the room to establish three hospitals ashore almost immediately after the landing. Until then, the hospital ships would handle serious cases. The hospital staffs allocated to the transports Birrell had ordered were equipped essentially to treat minor injuries.

The stalemate ashore, the priority given to tactical needs, and casualties vastly beyond those GHQ anticipated, emasculated these arrangements. The classification on the beach of casualties into seriously and lightly wounded broke down so that many lightly wounded were embarked on hospital ships and serious ones on the transports. Boatloads of wounded often went from one transport to another seeking accommodation. Both hospital ships and transports sailed to Alexandria (or Malta in the case of the *Somali*), sometimes only half full. Other transports, used to bring horses to the Peninsula, had them still on board. On one transport the wounded lay uncovered on the deck for the three nights the voyage took; on another four doctors had to treat 1600 casualties. Yet the well-equipped hospital ship *Hindoo* lay 'undiscovered' off Helles until 29 April![38] Birrell and his staff were incarcerated aboard *Arcadian*, out of touch with the battle and beyond Hamilton's reach. Conditions improved slowly, but for a few weeks, particularly at Anzac where the Gaba Tepe force went ashore, they were 'as bad as [those] . . . found by Florence Nightingale sixty years before at Scutari'.[39] Taylor's picture of a smiling and relaxed officer, gently being lowered onto a launch while immaculately dressed sailors look on, belies reality (p. 64).

By 27 April the British had some 20 000 troops ashore at Helles, opposed by about 6300 Turks in considerable disarray. So fatigue and approaching darkness were virtually the only real opposition facing the invaders as they advanced two miles up the Peninsula in brilliant evening sunshine that day. But they stopped before Achi Baba, the dominating ridge which should have been captured on the 25th. Looking like the head and shoulders of a heavyweight wrestler, that brooding, hulking height sits tantalizingly close in many of Taylor's photographs (e.g. p. 77). To the men at Helles it was 'as remote as Constantinople itself'.[40] On 29 April Hunter-Weston resumed the advance, hoping to capture Krithia, the village just short of Achi Baba, which the Plymouth battalion had found deserted on the first day. After four consecutive sleepless nights and many of them receiving their orders just before the attack, officers and men seemed to have little idea of what they were supposed to do. With only four guns ashore to support it, the assault quickly petered out even though some detachments briefly reached Krithia. Hamilton noted: 'Yesterday . . . I saw our men scatter right and left before an enemy they would have gone for with a cheer on the 25th or 26th.'[41] Rhodes James comments perceptively:

> The ramshackle, forgotten, but immensely significant First Battle of Krithia had signified the collapse of Hamilton's strategy . . . His army was spent, for the moment; Achi Baba . . . was as far away as ever; Turk reinforcements were being . . . deployed on the slopes of the mountain, with a marvellous view of the Allied lines straggling across the still green countryside.[42]

Since the landing, the MEF had lost over 9000, killed and wounded. On 1–2 May it was the Turks' turn to suffer. They launched a massive assault which the British and French, refreshed by three days of rest and proper food, repulsed—though not without difficulty. Two RND battalions were thrown into the battle when the French Senegalese broke under the Turk bombardment. Both battalions joined in the counter-attack next morning but 'the Turkish firing squad was waiting. We thought that, after the punishment we had given them during the night, they had moved out—but we were wrong'.[43]

Hamilton continued to batter away at Krithia, launching the Second and Third Battles in May and June respectively, followed by another series of extended operations in July. As Moorehead says: 'These battles were so repetitive, so ant-like and inconclusive, that it is almost impossible to discover any meaning in them unless one remembers the tremendous hopes with which each action was begun.'[44] At Second Krithia, the exhausted troops went forward at about the same time every day—11 a.m. on the 5th, 10 a.m. on the 7th and 10.15 a.m. on the 8th, by which evening 6000 men, thirty per cent of the attacking force, had been lost for a gain of 600 yards. Murray, not too pleased that his brigade had been attached to the French, wrote on 6 May:

> The Turkish fire was murderous . . . fewer men rose after each rush but we still charged forward blindly, repeatedly changing direction, but it did not appear to make the slightest difference. The fire was coming from all directions yet we could not see a single Turk or any sign of a trench.[45]

In the interval to 4 June, the RND participated in limited night advances which gained almost as much ground as the assaults of 6–8 May but at trifling cost. The opposing lines were now very close to each other. Better prepared than its predecessor but still lacking in artillery, the attack on 4 June was notable for the RND's use of eight armoured cars, part of the crazy collection of equipment the division found itself with on the Peninsula. This Third Battle of Krithia came close to success but Hunter-Weston committed his reserve in the RND and French sectors, where the attack was held up, instead of reinforcing those sectors where progress had been made. At dusk Murray, who led a charmed life, made his way back to the trench he had left near midday to find it

> three or four deep with bodies. They were slumped on the firestep and hanging over the parapet, some head first as they had died of their wounds or had been riddled with bullets as they were trying to make their escape. Of others, only their legs could be seen, their bodies lying over the parapet.[46]

An officer, who might have been describing any one of the Krithia battles or any attack on the Western Front for that matter, wrote of 4 June:

Our methods here seem to be based on a theory that all tactics are rot, and that the only way to do anything at all is to rush forward bald-headed minus support, minus reserves and in the end probably minus a limb or two.[47]

The RND had lost about 1400 men and its Collingwood Battalion, advancing 'as if on parade', was almost obliterated.[48] The remnants of the Collingwood were disbanded, together with the Benbow Battalion, to keep up the strength of the remaining naval units. Churchill, who had just resigned from the Admiralty, lamented to his brother: 'Poor Naval Division'.[49]

The attempt to advance at Helles had now cost the MEF nearly 60 000 casualties. But the attacks went on throughout June and July, the Turks losing almost 16 000 men themselves in counter-attacks between 28 June and 5 July. Hunter-Weston entrusted another major assault on 12–13 July to the RND before medical reports on the complete exhaustion of the division led him to revoke the order. Still, the RND was called upon for a last desperate assault on the second day, in which the Nelson Battalion lost almost 300 men. Relative to the numbers involved, this attack was the costliest of the Krithia/Achi Baba series. The 2nd Field Ambulance, the 3rd's sister unit, treated 2000 casualties on 14 July alone. Hunter-Weston, who had once remarked: 'Casualties? What do I care about casualties?' mentioned that he had been glad of the chance of 'blooding the pups'.[50] Having exhausted his army, he now collapsed from strain and sunstroke and left the Peninsula.

'Hunter-Bunter' and his conduct of the Helles battles evoke C. S. Forester's classic picture of the First World War generals, whom he likened to a group of savages debating how to extract a screw from a piece of wood: 'Accustomed only to nails, they had made one effort to pull out the screw by main force, and now that it had failed they were devising methods of applying more force still . . .'[51]

What then is to be said of Hamilton? The decision to make the supreme effort at Helles was his but he consistently refused to intervene in his subordinate's handling of the battle. Having given his last remaining reserve to Hunter-Weston before Second Krithia, 'all that was left to him of the high office of Commander-in-Chief was its load of responsibility'.[52] As he had before First Krithia, Hunter-Weston rejected Hamilton's suggestion that a dawn attack might offer better prospects. When the 42nd Division arrived in May, Hamilton grouped the three British divisions at Helles into the VIII Corps under Hunter-Weston's command. With this decision, Hamilton 'in effect formally surrendered all his powers to Hunter-Weston'.[53] At the end of July, a beach-head just over three miles deep by two wide represented the fruits of the Hamilton/Hunter-Weston policy. Krithia was still a mile beyond when the campaign ended. Summing up the fighting at Helles, John North commented: 'To the last [it] conformed to a singularly brainless and suicidal type of warfare'.[54]

Taylor's collection of photographs contains few of actual combat, although some of the views northwards towards Achi Baba may have been taken during the Krithia attacks (e.g. p. 77). But they are enough to convey some idea of the appalling prospect which confronted the infantry. The skies are invariably cloudless, except for the puff of shrapnel balls bursting in the air. The Turkish trenches are invisible, as are the deep irregular-shaped nullahs running off Achi Baba which divided Helles into roughly three equal sectors. Attacking across this completely exposed terrain, the infantry had to clear these nullahs of Turks as well as advance up the spurs between them. Marking the way forward to the front trenches were the ruined towers of a Roman aquaduct which used to carry water from Achi Baba to an earlier Sedd-el-Bahr. The army was trapped between the hill and the fort: 'it could go neither backward or forward. The plain, for all its openness, was a prison, which became a tomb'.[55]

One shot from this series (p. 68) shows the remnants of the Second Australian Brigade leaving W Beach for Anzac after Second Krithia. With the New Zealanders stalled on their left, the Australians had made the one worthwhile advance of the battle, charging up Krithia Spur into fire so intense that they moved with heads down, 'as if into fierce rain, some men holding their shovels before their faces like umbrellas in a thunderstorm'.[56] The Australians were unimpressed by the RND, whose troops they met when the Royal Marine Brigade and the Nelson Battalion were sent to their cramped one-square-mile beach-head at Anzac on 28–29 April. The Australians were dismayed by the sight of the newcomers' pale, slender physiques crowned with pith helmets and, after several incidents, concluded that they were jumpy.[57] The Marines acquired from their initials the epithets 'Royal Malingerers' and 'Run My Lads Imshi'.[58] 'The only real advantage we gained', remembered one soldier in General Monash's Fourth Brigade, 'was that they brought several machine guns with them'.[59] Birdwood, the commander at Anzac, considered the RND troops to be 'nearly useless', an opinion which the commander of the Marines, Brigadier-General Trotman, shared, according to Monash, whose sector the Marines were reinforcing.[60] Taylor does not appear to have visited Anzac, although the RND passed it on its way to Helles after the feint at Bulair.

At both Helles and Anzac, the infantryman's routine followed the pattern it has always had in war. Moments of extreme terror punctuated much longer periods when the danger was less acute. From Orchard Gully on the right of the British sector, where the 3rd Field Ambulance eventually went ashore, Taylor captured this routine superbly during visits to the RND's trenches in lulls between attacks.

Like it did on the Western Front, day began as it ended, with a stand-to, when all men stood with rifles on the firesteps of their trenches, ready to repel any attempt by the Turks to take advantage of the change from night to day routine and vice versa. A photo taken near the end of the campaign at Fusilier Bluff sets the scene (p. 94). The men are dressed irregularly. Some have towels wrapped around their heads while one sports the pith helmet which the RND wore when it left Avonmouth in February. Steel helmets, which would have saved countless lives at Gallipoli (and on the Western Front), were not issued until February 1916. Because digging was very hard on this rocky height, the men have deepened their trench by building it up with sandbags. Items of personal kit and the ubiquitous rum jar lie on the ground behind them.

After an officer had checked fields of fire, the condition of the trench and the serviceability of weapons and stores, the men would be stood down, leaving one or more per platoon to keep watch on the Turkish line opposite. Those not on sentry would be allocated jobs—fetching ammunition, stores and rations from the beach, improving existing trenches or digging new ones. Bruckshaw records that he was digging at least every second day throughout July.[61] Some men would 'rest' but were still liable to be called upon for fatigue duties. Taylor captured them sitting on their improvised trench seats, chatting, smoking and reading magazines (p. 91). Their rifles are at the ready nearby, resting on sandbags and pointing towards the Turkish lines. Machine-guns were continually manned and trained on selected points in the Turkish trenches or rear areas. Taylor shows one gunner wearing headphones (p. 89). His fire may have been corrected by forward observers whose adjustments would be signalled to him. Perhaps the soldier looking through the telescope was engaged on such a task (p. 88).

Most of the trench shots in the collection depict the Plymouth Avenue area in the sector which the RND held on the extreme right of the British line, alongside the French (pp. 91–3). Plymouth Avenue conveys a sense of tidiness and order. Dugouts cut into the sides of trench walls offer some protection from shelling and the weather. Rifles stand neatly in rests also cut into the trench wall, which is almost perfectly formed. Sandbags bolster weakened sections of the parapet. Constant pounding by hundreds of pairs of feet has compacted the trench floor.

Yet the trench appears to be linear, without the frequent traverses which prevented an attacker firing down its length and minimized the effect of shells bursting in it. And the trench is spotless, unlike those at Fusilier Bluff, or the line between Gully Ravine and Krithia Nullah, which the RND took over in mid-August. The latter was once a Turkish trench and the bodies of British and Turkish soldiers were built into the hastily constructed trench walls. Sometimes a burst of machine-gun fire would shatter a section of the parapet, dumping a shower of maggots onto those sheltering in the dugouts below. Still, while Plymouth Avenue may be slightly unreal, it does bring out the numbing effect of trench warfare, which affected soldiers on the Peninsula and on the Western Front in the same way:

> no-one had been prepared for vigilant inaction, for the blinded feeling which followed being confined below the surface, for the demoralizing stooped walk, for the need to take constant care. Men were worn out by all these things and, released from the need to polish buttons and salute, they dropped their weapons, lost their kit, slept on sentry, urinated in the trenches, cried when put in a listening post, 'forgot' everything they were told . . .[62]

Night brought little relief. Indeed, it was the most active period of the twenty-four hours. Patrols went out and the work of fatigue parties increased to complete the repair and portage jobs which were too hazardous to undertake by day. For the soldier on watch, night brought isolation and fear as his imagination turned innocent objects into marauding Turks. All the time the soldier had to fight to stay awake. A. P. Herbert, who belonged to the RND, observed:

> The men fell asleep with their heads against the iron loopholes, and, starting up as the officer shook them, swore that they had never nodded. Only by constant movement could the officer be sure even of himself . . .[63]

At the end of one watch, a distraught Bruckshaw 'could scarcely see at all'.[64]

Like most troops on the Peninsula, the RND had received little training in trench warfare. The Hawke Battalion, for example, had only had one day's training in England on trench digging.[65] Disadvantaging the MEF further was the lack of suitable equipment for trench combat, which spawned a frenzied spree of improvisation amply demonstrated in several of Taylor's photographs (pp. 86, 90).

Soldiers are seen observing no man's land through home-made trench periscopes, much like those football fans use to see over the heads of a crowd. The invention of the periscope rifle, in which the periscope was fixed to the rifle, enabling the firer to aim and shoot without raising his head above the parapet, helped counter the Turkish sniper menace. The Turks possessed bombs (the most important weapon for close-in trench fighting) in abundance and were trained in their use at von Sanders's insistence. The MEF initially had only the bomb and bomb-thrower hastily invented just before the campaign by Mr Garland, an official at the Cairo arsenal. The scarcity and limited effectiveness of these devices led to the manufacture on W Beach of a 'jam-tin' bomb, comprising gelignite, detonators and a slow burning fuse in a jam-tin filled with bullets and shrapnel. These were thrown by hand but for longer ranges catapults were used. They consisted of ten or twelve lengths of rubber fitted to each end of two arms, with the other ends attached to a wire and canvas basket for the bomb. But the elastic continually broke and the accuracy of the bomb relied more on good luck than good judgement. Trench mortars were also in short supply, although, in this respect at least, the MEF was better off than the Turks. One of their mortars came from the Constantinople Museum where it had lain for years gathering dust.

Behind the trenches, Helles was undergoing a transformation. The extent is clearly evident from a comparison between Taylor's first shots of the beaches (e.g. p. 56) and those he took later in the campaign (pp. 59–61). Compton Mackenzie likened the scene then to 'a seaside resort on a fine bank holiday':

> Even the aeroplane on the top of the low cliff eastward had the look of an 'amusement' to provide a sixpenny or threepenny thrill; the tents might so easily conceal phrenologists or fortune tellers; the signal station might well be a camera obscura; the very carts of the Indian Transport, seen through the driven sand, had an air of waiting goat carriages.[66]

At V Beach, the old French battleship *Massena* had been sunk a quarter of a mile west of the *River Clyde* to form a miniature harbour in the bay. Sedd-el-Bahr castle now served as an ammunition depot, while a road cut by Turkish prisoners and a light railway ran along the shore to the cliffs at Helles, past stores arranged in immaculate piles. Forage for horses and mules was stacked high to reduce the effects of shellfire. W Beach was similar, Hamilton describing it as 'An ant's nest in revolution'.[67] Floating piers were improvised from the wreckage of lighters and ships' boats. Further west, Gully Ravine had also become a storehouse and administrative centre, complete with stables, medical facilities and temporary cemeteries. From about five miles out to sea, a cloud of yellowish dust was visible above the tip of the Peninsula in the early summer months. Two miles closer to the shore the first whiffs of decaying flesh were noticeable.[68]

The scene offshore had also changed, although the difference is not reflected in any of Taylor's photographs. On 12–13 May, a Turkish torpedo boat sank HMS *Goliath*. Then on 25 May, the German submarine *U21* despatched a second battleship, HMS *Triumph*, in full view of both armies at Anzac. Ten days later, *U21* treated Helles to a similar spectacle by sinking yet another, HMS *Majestic*, which left part of her ram above the water after she turned turtle.

Although the Germans were unable to repeat these successes, no Allied ship felt safe again. The battleships were withdrawn and only emerged thereafter when actually required to support the army. Greater activity by cruisers and destroyers, and the arrival on 4 July of four monitors mounting fourteen-inch guns, eventually compensated for their removal but nonetheless, the effect on morale was significant. Large transports were forbidden to sail from Mudros to the Peninsula, adding to the sense of abandonment that ran through the MEF. The *Arcadian*, still off W Beach with Hamilton finally aboard, sailed to the island of Imbros, eighteen miles from Helles and fifteen from Anzac. GHQ established itself there on 31 May. Hamilton, too, emerged only for special reasons, which effectively gave even more control to the local commanders.

The recall of the battleships left the Turkish artillery on the Asiatic shore (collectively christened 'Asiatic Annie') largely unmolested during June and July. Shelling from these guns against the beaches and rear areas at Helles increased and was particularly severe in the sectors held by the French and the RND on the right flank. Because of the small size of the beach-head, troops were never able to escape it, even when they were in so-called rest areas. The RND's rest camps were directly behind their trench sector and provided flimsy protection, owing to the scarcity of the timber and corrugated iron needed to construct shelters. Some 'resting' battalions occasionally suffered as many casualties in 24 hours as a battalion in the front line. Bruckshaw referred frequently to Asiatic Annie and as far as he was concerned, she did 'a lot of damage'.[69] His opinion illustrates the effect the shelling had on men's nerves because, for the most part, it did little serious damage at all.[70]

Unlike the Western Front, there were no safe areas behind the lines at Gallipoli. The 3rd Field Ambulance's location at Orchard Gully was within a stone's throw of the front line. As a surgeon, Taylor faced many more of the infantryman's dangers than he would have in France and not just from artillery. Spent bullets struck the field ambulance, as they did the rest camps. German aircraft were sometimes troublesome, Bruckshaw observing on 22 June 'A bit of a scrap between one of our aeroplanes and a Taube before breakfast. It got away and returned after breakfast and dropped bombs on our camp'.[71] Another tried to bomb the kite balloon used for naval gunfire spotting, which Taylor photographed in quieter times ascending from the balloon ship *Hector* (p. 45). One of his most remarkable pictures shows a bomb exploding on the cliffs while the bomber, no more than a blur, makes its escape (p. 121).

The heat was enervating for all troops. By July it was averaging 84°F in the shade—if any could be found. Helles was 'parched and dry and every blade of herbage had disappeared'.[72] The Peninsula resembled a desert, brown and ankle-deep in dust. Between 4 a.m. and 8 p.m. every trench and dugout became a furnace, which the occupants shared with scorpions, centipedes and tarantulas brought out by the heat. Whereas the Turks on the heights had abundant water supplies, shortages on the plain below were acute. Apart from one or two in Gully Ravine, Helles was devoid of wells. Water had to be brought from Egypt, 700 miles away, pumped ashore and carried forward by mules.[73]

Notwithstanding the jollity of the 3rd Field Ambulance's officers as Taylor snapped them dining at an improvised table in their open-air mess (p. 109), men's spirits were lowered by the monotony of the diet. It consisted of various combinations of bully beef, bacon, cheese, hard biscuits and apricot jam, which the heat rendered almost inedible. The bully could be poured like treacle from its tin onto plates too hot to touch, while the jam was more like a syrupy juice. The flies, which bred rapidly in the unsanitary conditions, were regarded as a worse enemy than the Turks. Murray described their onslaught as he opened a tin of jam:

> the flies are so thick that they are squashed in the process. One never sees the jam; one can only see a blue-black mixture of sticky, sickly flies. They drink the sweat on our bodies and our lips and eyes are always covered with them. As we wipe them away, we squash them, thereby making more moisture for the others that take their place. There is no escape from them. The hundreds we eat do not seem to lessen the swarm. They are forever present, night and day.[74]

The photograph of soldiers in their primitive gas hoods (p. 110) probably shows them using these devices as protection against flies rather than for a gas drill.[75] A piece of muslin, which he could put over his face when he slept or ate, became one of the most precious possessions a soldier could have. Jerrold wrote of the Peninsula at this time as

> a place where a burning sun had turned the bodies of the slain to a premature corruption, where there was no resting-place free from physical contamination, where the air, the surface of the ground, and the soil beneath the surface were alike poisonous, fetid, corrupt.[76]

Proper canteens selling small luxuries to vary the diet, shops, concerts, YMCA tents, civilian contact—particularly with females—and other measures which might have offered some respite from these privations did not exist on the Peninsula as they did in France. Moorehead comments: 'the very absence of these pleasures created another scale of values'.[77] The evening cuppa, sharing a parcel from home, improving dugouts, picking lice out of clothing and talking of what one would do when it was all over, assumed almost mystical importance. But the main joy was sea bathing as Taylor's photographs clearly show (e.g. p. 111). Throughout the day the coast would be dotted with naked men enjoying a refreshing splash in the Aegean even though they risked Turkish shelling. Birdwood spoke for most when he said he would 'rather be knocked out clean than live dirty'.[78]

Not until mid-June, with the arrival of the 52nd Division, were the first troops able to leave the Peninsula for a rest. Units of the MEF were then spelled at camps on Imbros and later, Mudros. But neither island was adequately equipped with the recreational facilities needed to compensate for the lack of leave further afield, such as London or Paris, that the troops on the Western Front enjoyed. The flies were still omnipresent and the heat was stifling, while on Imbros the guns at Anzac were audible. Moreover, the experience of some troops at the hands of the Lines of Communication (LOC) staff at Mudros, who were responsible for administering the camps, led them to long for Gallipoli.

As usual, much of the confusion on Imbros and Mudros stemmed from Hamilton's indifference towards administrative matters. The physical separation of the GHQ administrative staff on Imbros from the LOC staff at Mudros prevented effective co-ordination between them. Troops derisively referred to 'Imbros, Mudros and Chaos!' Comfortably ensconced aboard the *Aragon*, the LOC staff were a byword for inefficiency, which was reduced but not eliminated when Hamilton finally reorganized the LOC arrangements in July. Even then, Hamilton was reluctant to allot resources for the development of Mudros because he believed that the bridge-heads on the Peninsula would eventually become large enough to assume some of its functions.[79] Thus Monash arrived at Mudros in September to find that no tents had been provided for his sick and understrength brigade. It was promptly drenched by heavy thunderstorms. As for the LOC staff on the *Aragon*:

> They told us that they were going to do, oh, such a lot to make us thoroughly comfortable! They gave us some travelling kitchens. They came a few days after and took them away at very short notice, and told us to requisition for dixies . . .[80]

The combination of depressing conditions, tiring work under shellfire, grossly inadequate spells out of the line, food that men would rather throw away than eat and, above all, the flies, made the onset of intestinal disease certain. By July the 'Gallipoli Gallop', or the 'Gallipoli Trots' as it was alternatively known, had reached epidemic proportions: 'there was scarcely a man . . . who was not a victim'.[81] With an average of over one thousand men being evacuated weekly, the disease was causing far greater losses than the Turks were.[82] Hamilton remarked on the overwhelming lassitude it engendered: 'It fills me with a desperate longing to lie down and do nothing but rest . . . and this I think, must be the reason the Greeks were ten long years in taking Troy.'[83] Some soldiers barely had the strength to drag themselves to the latrines, where they stayed until they died through loss of blood and intestine or from Turkish shellfire. Murray's poignant description of the RND was typical of the MEF as a whole:

> It is pitiful to see men, not long ago strong and healthy, now with drawn faces and staring eyes, struggling towards the firing line. Most of them should be in hospital. They are cheating death but only just. They are walking corpses—the ghosts of Gallipoli.[84]

Whether Taylor had dysentery and if so, to what extent, is unknown. But he would certainly have been confronted with the consequences of the medical services' lamentable handling of the epidemic. At first contaminated water was suspected as the source; when the realization dawned that the flies were the main cause, the outbreak was beyond control. The lack of wood and corrugated iron prevented the construction of flyproof kitchens and latrines. The kitchen Taylor photographed at Helles (p. 107) is completely open, while latrines usually consisted of a hole in the ground with a pole to hang on to. Birrell rejected the Anzac doctors' request for oil and chlorinated lime and instead suggested suspending fly papers from bushes and the incineration of excreta and rubbish. His first proposal was ludicrous, his second largely forbidden because the Turks registered their guns on smoke rising from the British lines.[85] As late as August, Birrell attributed the dysentery at Anzac to sea bathing.[86]

By this time Mudros had become an important hospital centre. The 2nd Royal Naval Hospital, which Taylor photographed in January 1916 (p. 35), was typical of its facilities. Nine such hospitals had opened there since the end of May as well as convalescent depots and additional field ambulances. But water supply on Mudros was always a problem, while some of the hospitals were poorly sited and lacked adequate accommodation and suitable landing places. So sick and wounded arriving at Mudros were often transshipped straight to waiting transports which sailed before the patient could be properly classified. Hospitals in Malta and Egypt quickly filled to overflowing, as they did at the time of the landing.

In June Surgeon-General Babtie had arrived from India as Principal Director of Medical Services in the Mediterranean. He altered Birrell's scheme to allow hospital ships to sail to a set timetable rather than when full. Even with the use of 'black ships'—additional transports used for casualty evacuation but not flying the red cross—the new plan proved unable to cope. Into the argument between Birrell and Babtie stepped Surgeon-General Sir James Porter, appointed against the wishes of Hamilton and Babtie as Hospital Transport Officer with complete control over the despatch of all ships used for casualty evacuation, but without any responsibility to GHQ. So the new scheme Porter introduced was difficult to co-ordinate and quickly broke down. Not until November, when Porter's appointment was abolished and a satisfactory balance struck between the military, naval and medical staffs over the responsibility for casualty evacuation, did the plight of the wounded improve. As always at Gallipoli, the change came too late. J. G. Gasparich, who was a dysentery patient sent to Imbros in this period with dozens of others in like state, wrote: 'we slept on the ground and were fed stew and tea which only made matters worse'.[87] Bruckshaw reached Mudros on 27 October. During his six-week stay, a group of nurses arrived who improved the hospital until it 'became somewhat more worthy of the name of hospital'.[88]

The abject physical state of the MEF helps to explain the failure of Hamilton's last desperate throw at Gallipoli. In June three divisions were sent to the Peninsula, followed by two more in July. Hamilton had already decided to transfer his main effort from Helles to Anzac.[89] Feints at both on 6 August would herald a breakout by Birdwood's force to the north of Anzac to capture the crests of the Sari Bair range. Heavy guns and searchlights subsequently installed on them would prevent Turkish use of the Straits and render their positions across the Peninsula untenable. In the meantime, Lieutenant-General F. W. Stopford's IX Corps would land at Suvla, three miles north, to seize guns troubling Anzac and to protect Birdwood's flank as his units carried out the main operation. A. J. Hill says: 'Hamilton's offensive in August, by reason of its scale, its complexity and the importance of its aim, was one of the great battles of the war.'[90]

What followed was a repetition of events at the landing, in that further lapses of command let slip the fruits of early success. The feint at Lone Pine at Anzac very nearly broke through the Turkish lines, the Suvla landing was virtually uncontested, the battle for the Sari Bair heights was for some time delicately poised. But Hamilton again stood aloof at critical junctures. He had agreed when the elderly Stopford, who had little experience of fighting and none of command in battle, argued that his main task should be to establish Suvla as a base rather than to help Birdwood. So the IX Corps remained on its peaceful beaches where the men were swimming. Not until thirty-six hours after they went ashore did Hamilton, still at Imbros, urge Stopford to move forward. But the interlude had allowed the Turks to reinforce and they threw IX Corps back across the Suvla Plain.

The commanders at Anzac were also out of touch with their battle, confidently predicting to Hamilton on 9 August, during his first visit to Anzac since the offensive started, that the heights would be theirs next day. In fact the attack had already failed. 'All that remained was aftermath', says Rhodes James.[91] It consisted of the hideously bloody fighting around Hill 60 which eventually linked the Suvla beach-head, six miles wide and three deep, with Anzac. The MEF had lost over 40 000 men in under three weeks.

Apart from the detachment to Suvla of the Anson Battalion to be in charge of pack transport, and of the 2nd Field Ambulance to supplement the IX Corps' medical resources, the RND took no part in the August offensive. Murray was grateful to be an onlooker in the diversionary attacks which General Street, Hunter-Weston's equally optimistic and bullish successor, launched on 6–7 August. They cost the 29th and 42nd Divisions 3600 men. 'Just like old times,' Murray wrote.[92]

By now the RND's strength was down to 129 officers and 5038 men, of whom 'not ten per cent would have been considered fit in France for duty in the quietest part of the line'.[93] The last straw came with an order to transfer 350 fleet reserve stokers for fleet service. Their loss left several of the depleted battalions without most of their regular ratings. In the reorganization which was necessary to accommodate their departure, heavy battle casualties and the crippling losses through disease, the four Marine battalions were amalgamated into two. They then joined the Howe and Anson Battalions in the new Second Naval Brigade. The remaining two battalions of the old Second Naval Brigade joined the Drake and Hawke Battalions to restore the First Naval Brigade to a four battalion formation.[94]

The post-August period saw no serious fighting. Saps were pushed out, barricades moved forward and shelling endured. The fly plague, and with it the ravages of dysentery, began to abate with the onset of colder weather in October. Taylor's photographs of himself outside his dugout and of two other officers standing above the water (frontispiece and p. 122), all heavily clothed, contrast sharply with the scenes of naked men cavorting in the sea a few months before. Taylor and the two officers were among the fortunate ones because not all of the winter stores and protective clothing had arrived. Typically, one consignment was returned in error to Mudros.

The RND had almost completed a new rest camp on the extreme left of Helles which promised unaccustomed comfort and safety, when a blizzard struck the Peninsula on 27 November, followed by snow next day. Murray wrote afterwards:

> we were amazed at the devastation around us; it was unbelievable. In the vast quagmire, hundreds of men stood stupefied and shivering in the uncanny silence. A few hours ago it would have been fatal to expose oneself above the earthworks for a fraction of a second, yet here we were, oblivious of danger, just standing in the open, bewildered. The elements had beaten us.[95]

About 1200 men were evacuated with frostbite and exposure from Helles but almost 15 000 were afflicted at Anzac and Suvla. Most of the 280 deaths came from the northern enclaves. The Turks fared worse and, occasionally, both sides stamped about trying to keep warm in full view of each other with few shots being fired.

Shortly before the blizzard, the 3rd Field Ambulance moved to its winter quarters above X Beach, where it amalgamated with the 2nd Field Ambulance to form the X Beach Ambulance. Taylor took several photographs of the construction of the dugouts along Officers' Walk which show them to be sturdily built of materials almost unobtainable on the Peninsula previously (pp. 116–20). His own dugout was weatherproof and well-appointed, boasting a homemade stove, curtains, and improvised shelving (p. 72). Taylor added personal touches such as books, pictures and slippers by his ornately quilted bed. Other shots include the Officers' Mess, possibly during celebrations for Christmas or for Taylor's 32nd birthday (p. 120).

When the RND took over the French sector above Morto Bay early in December, the men were amazed to find that dugouts like Taylor's were commonplace. Expecting facilities less sanitary and more primitive than their own, they discovered that the trenches and dugouts were deeper and roofed over with splinter-proof corrugated iron manufactured in England. Jerrold commented bitterly:

> This was not Sybaritic luxury. It merely meant that the French War Office had sent out to Gallipoli supplies of stores essential to the health and comfort, and so to the fighting efficiency, of the troops, in quantities which were proportioned to the numbers of their expeditionary force. For English troops, corresponding supplies had never been available.[96]

Nor would they be in the future, for the campaign was drawing to a close. The government, irritated by Hamilton's optimism and fast losing confidence in him, had recalled him in mid-October. The immediate cause of Hamilton's fall was his emotional response when Kitchener sought his views on the possibility of evacuation. Hamilton's estimate of casualties ranged from half his force to 'a real catastrophe'.[97] His successor, General Sir Charles Monro, had commanded the British Third Army in France and was a dedicated 'Westerner', who believed the war could only be won on the Western Front. Shocked by the precariousness of the Allied positions on the Peninsula and mindful of the effects of winter and the expected arrival of German heavy guns, he recommended withdrawal. Kitchener reluctantly agreed when he visited Gallipoli in November. The last troops left Anzac and Suvla on 19–20 December. Murray was stunned: 'Had we really admitted defeat? Had all the suffering been wasted and what of the dead?'[98]

Helles was to be held for the moment, although preparations for its evacuation were well underway. The deception plan was as imaginative as in the earlier withdrawal. Every effort was made to maintain normal levels of activity even as the embarkation began early in January. Men marched in full view of the Turks on the open roads, no camps were struck and firing continued routinely. Dummies, like those Taylor photographed (p. 123), were ready to take the place of the men as they left. But von Sanders, embarrassed by the bloodless escape at Anzac and Suvla, had ordered a close watch to be kept on Helles. By 7 January, its garrison totalled 16 000 of whom 4400 were RND troops. On that day the Turks attacked after the heaviest bombardment of the campaign. Supported by warships, the defenders' fire was devastating and only at two points did the Turks leave their trenches.

On the following night in a rising storm, the last troops left the Peninsula as the British magazines exploded in a blinding sheet of flame. Not one man was lost. This success, carried out before an expectant enemy mounting vigorous activity, was 'nothing short of astonishing'.[99] Liddell Hart judged that 'the skill with which our forces were extricated is the one thing that extracts the sting of defeat'.[100] To which Murray's final words might well be added: 'The Turks did not beat us—we were beaten by our High Command.'[101] Total MEF casualties were about 265 000, including 46 000 dead. The Turks lost about 300 000.[102]

When the RND reached Mudros on 10 January, it reverted to naval command. The First Royal Naval Brigade established semi-permanent garrisons on Imbros and Tenedos as well as on Mudros. The routine consisted of 'a certain amount of police work, the examination of persons passing in and out of the small area in occupation of the garrison, the mounting of numerous guards and pickets and the search for hostile snipers whenever someone threw a blank cartridge into an incinerator'.[103]

The Second Royal Naval Brigade was lent to the Salonika Army for duty on the Gulf of Stavros. At French instigation, Britain and France had hastily sent an expedition to Salonika in October to aid Serbia. But Serbia eventually fell to a combined Austro-German and Bulgarian stroke. Their prestige among the Balkan states dented by the Dardanelles failure, the Allies were reluctant to withdraw. By holding Salonika they could bolster Greece and aid Rumania if, as expected, she declared war on the Triple Alliance. But the Allies mounted no serious offensive on this front until late 1918. Content to leave the Bulgarians guarding it, the Germans called Salonika ' "their largest internment camp" and with half a million Allied troops locked up their gibe had some justification . . .'.[104]

Stavros formed the extreme right of an Allied line sixty miles long. The Second Royal Naval Brigade was charged with improving the defences in its sector and intercepting Greek stragglers.[105] Bruckshaw disliked Stavros, complaining about the living conditions and the hard work—as always, digging.[106] But this inactive theatre enabled the RND to recuperate from the Gallipoli campaign. Taylor took full advantage of the peaceful environment, wandering freely over the rugged countryside and talking to the Greek peasants whose way of life had been the same for centuries. His photograph of the bearer division of the 2nd Field Ambulance (p. 126) and the hospital at Rendina Gorge (p. 125) portray a unit that had regained its verve. The picture of the mounted officer staring out over the long reeds of Lake Besika (p. 128) suggests a man wondering what fate had in store for him. Taylor probably wondered as well.

The answer was not long in coming. In May 1916 the RND arrived on the Western Front, where it participated in every major action subsequently mounted by the British Expeditionary Force. Its losses there amounted to 34 992 all ranks in just over two years, as compared to 7198 in eight months at Gallipoli.[107] Taylor left the division well before the

23

Armistice but not as a casualty. He joined HMS *Vivid* in February 1917 and transferred to the Royal Air Force in June 1918. Bruckshaw was killed in April 1917 during the Battle of Arras. As he has no known grave, his name is inscribed on the wall of the Arras Memorial to the Missing. Murray survived the war.

In contrast to the baleful depression evoked by the campaign on the Western Front, an aura of romance has blossomed over Gallipoli even though it, too, was one of the war's great tragedies. The reasons are not hard to find. The Dardanelles is an area of immense historical richness. The ancient Hellespont, it was the scene of the siege of Troy and Xerxes' crossing by a bridge of boats to invade Greece in 480 BC. Leander is supposed to have swum the Narrows every night to meet the priestess Hero; Lord Byron did swim it in 1810. Except in high summer, the area is exquisitely beautiful. Aspinall-Oglander could write during a lull in the Second Battle of Krithia:

> The grassy slopes that crown the cliffs are carpeted with flowers. The azure sky is cloudless; the air is fragrant with the scent of wild thyme. In front, beyond a smiling valley studded with cypress and olive and patches of young corn, the ground rises gently to the village of Krithia, standing amidst clumps of mulberry and oak . . . Away to the right, edged with a ribbon of silvery sand, lie the sapphire arc of Morto Bay, the glistening Dardanelles, and the golden fields of Troy. On the left, a mile out in the Aegean, a few warships lie motionless, like giants asleep, their gaunt outlines mirrored in a satin sea; while behind them, in the tender haze of the horizon, is the delicately pencilled outline of snow-capped Samothrace. As far as the eye can see there is no sign of movement; the world seems bathed in sleep.[108]

Furthermore, the struggle was fit to rank alongside any ancient epic. Cyril Falls remarks:

> Ordinary bravery withstands smashing bombardments and will charge under withering fires. To maintain the ability to do this in the conditions under which British, French, Australians, New Zealanders, Indians, Turks, and a handful of Germans lived on the Gallipoli peninsula is a far different thing. Men who have looked since at the tiny ledges, a few yards from the Turkish trenches, from which companies never moved in daylight, have held their breath and marvelled.[109]

Gallipoli was also the only campaign which offered the chance of a quick, dramatic victory. Unlike on the Western Front, the objectives whose capture would have ensured success were always visible. As Peter Liddle says, Achi Baba and Sari Bair were 'so tantalizingly close'.[110] And whereas on the Western Front the domination of science made warfare impersonal, the opposite was true on the Peninsula, where innovation and ingenuity flourished. Finally, as their first major national endeavour, Gallipoli was instrumental in forging the national identity of Australia and New Zealand. In the process, soldiers from those two dominions enriched the English language with the word ANZAC.

Twenty-one years after the campaign, John North ventured the opinion that 'as Gallipoli will always remain one of the great true stories of the world' it was sufficient reason for telling it again.[111] North was justifying his own contribution to the already large library of works—British, French, Turkish and German, fiction and non-fiction—that the campaign had already inspired. His view was also remarkably prescient, although the title of his own book, *Gallipoli: The Fading Vision*, suggests that North himself had little idea of what the future held. Each generation has felt the need to retell the story. As late as 1967, Gallipoli veterans in the United Kingdom founded the Gallipoli Association. They are vastly outnumbered today by members born long after the campaign. Over seventy years on, interest in Gallipoli shows no sign of fading.

Although there are obvious traces of battle in the rugged hills of Anzac, few signs of what Taylor photographed at Helles survive today. The shattered hulk of Sedd-el-Bahr stands sentinel at V Beach. A gun barrel lies in the sand and is being slowly corroded by the sea. Little dimples in the grassy slopes above the beach are all that remain of the trenches from which the Turks engaged the invader. A Turkish radar station overlooks W Beach and the sentries give one every encouragement to stay away. Nothing remains of Officers' Walk above X Beach. But in the waters off the beaches, the rusting remains of lighters can be discerned when the tide is out. A walk towards the still forbidding outline of Achi Baba reveals traces of the dugouts which housed the 3rd Field Ambulance in Orchard Gully and the Roman viaduct. The most obvious reminders of what happened here are the memorials, British, French and Turkish, and the cemeteries, lovingly maintained by the Commonwealth War Graves Commission.[112] A wander amongst the headstones might evoke Hamilton's eulogy to those who served under him:

> You will hardly fade away until the sun fades out of the sky and the earth sinks into universal blackness. For already you form part of that great tradition of the Dardanelles which began with Hector and Achilles. In another few thousand years the two stories will have blended into one, and whether when 'the iron roaring went up to the vault of heaven through the unharvested sky' as Homer tells us, it was the spear of Achilles or whether it was a 100 lb. shell from Asiatic Annie won't make much odds to the Almighty.[113]

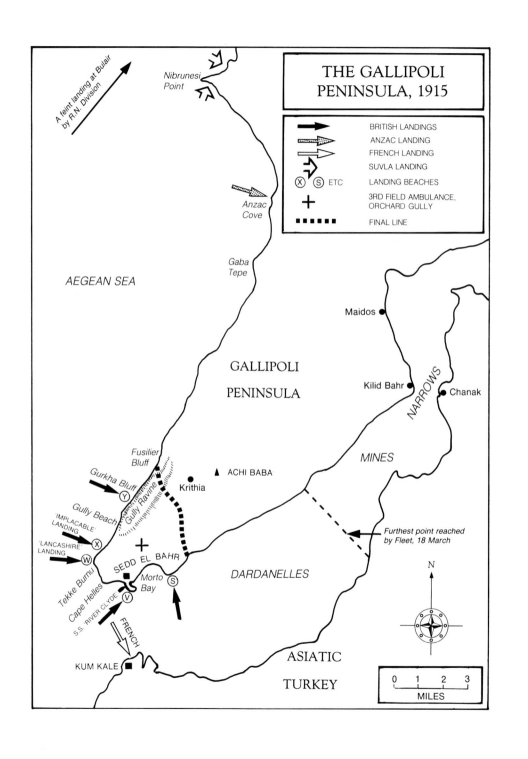

THE GALLIPOLI
PENINSULA, 1915

BRITISH LANDINGS
ANZAC LANDING
FRENCH LANDING
SUVLA LANDING
(X) (S) ETC   LANDING BEACHES
3RD FIELD AMBULANCE,
ORCHARD GULLY
FINAL LINE

A feint landing at Bulair
by R.N. Division

Nibrunesi
Point

Anzac
Cove

Gaba
Tepe

AEGEAN SEA

Maidos

GALLIPOLI

PENINSULA

Kilid Bahr

NARROWS

Chanak

MINES

Fusilier
Bluff

▲ ACHI BABA

Gurkha Bluff

Y

Krithia

Gully Beach

'IMPLACABLE'
LANDING

Gully Ravine

Furthest point reached
by Fleet, 18 March

X

'LANCASHIRE'
LANDING

W

N

Tekke Burnu

SEDD EL BAHR

DARDANELLES

Cape Helles

Morto
Bay

S

V

S.S. 'RIVER CLYDE'

FRENCH

ASIATIC

KUM KALE

TURKEY

0   1   2   3
MILES

RND troops embarking at Avonmouth for Mudros in February 1915. The orders sending the RND overseas came as a surprise to the division. They arrived on 29 January, the day after most of the RND had completed its concentration at Blandford camp for divisional training. The first units of the RND sailed on 6 February, their destination still secret. Many rumours said they were headed for East Africa.

RND machine-gun officers getting acquainted with their Barr and Stroud rangefinders. They would have few opportunities to use them on the Peninsula because the well-camouflaged Turkish positions were largely invisible from the Allied lines.

A group of men at physical training while an officer relaxes and does his best not to notice. The cramped conditions aboard a troopship limited training to physical fitness sessions and to activities suited to the classroom, such as instruction on weapons and in map-reading. But what the RND really lacked was field training at brigade and divisional level. Some officers considered that its battalion training was inadequate as well. The suddenness of the RND's departure had precluded this advanced training, thus handicapping the division throughout the Gallipoli campaign.

The ramparts of Malta's Grand Harbour with the city of Valetta behind them. RND private, Horace Bruckshaw, was struck by the absence of chimneys on the houses and by the stand-up rowing style of the hawkers in their small boats. At dusk, the firing of a salute and the playing of the British and French national anthems by ships' bands signalled the lowering of the colours. Searchlights lit up the harbour at night. Malta was an important source of ammunition and wharfage at the start of the campaign and an important medical centre throughout.

Port Said, where the RND began the transhipment of its stores at the end of March. Lack of foresight and care in the original loading in England forced the RND to unload every one of its fourteen transports at Port Said and rearrange their cargoes according to tactical requirements. On 3 April, General Sir Ian Hamilton inspected the RND in its desert camp outside the town. Before they left Port Said on 7 April, some RND units were attached to the Suez Canal defences for a brief spell of training under field conditions.

Even to the most philistine of men, the Pyramids and the Sphinx held an inexorable fascination as timeless reminders of an ancient past. Rare was the soldier in Cairo who did not make the short trip outside the city to see them. As the RND was never camped near Cairo, Taylor probably took this photograph, and the one following, while on leave there. Leave would have been much easier for Taylor to get as an officer than for a private like Bruckshaw.

A Cairo back street. The sights, sounds and smells of the city, its contrasts, and the contact with an unfamiliar culture, were exciting stimuli to those men who had never previously left their own shores. Stimulus of a different sort (and for many, just as exciting as the Egyptian cultural experience) was available in the red-light Wasser district. Seeking revenge on those whom they felt had 'gyped' them or infected them or both, Australian troops rioted in the Wasser on Good Friday 1915.

Transports assembling in Mudros Harbour, Lemnos, after the reorganization in Egypt. This photograph shows the bleakness of Lemnos and the absence of port facilities. Even a moderate breeze turned the exposed waters choppy and it sometimes took several hours to row back to a ship from the shore.

Mudros transformed. A light railway services the 2nd Royal Naval Hospital at Mudros in January 1916. Mudros accommodated nine such hospitals and numerous lesser installations at this time as opposed to the solitary hospital established there before the campaign began. But safe landing facilities were still lacking, and the featureless terrain left the camps, both hutted and under canvas, terribly exposed to the gales which frequently battered the island.

The RND training in Trebuki Bay, on the island of Skyros, shortly before sailing for the Dardanelles. The 3rd Field Ambulance practised setting up a dressing station and moving over ground more rugged than the terrain on Lemnos. Rupert Brooke was buried in an olive grove above Trebuki Bay; Asquith, Freyberg, Shaw-Stewart and Denys Browne were among those at his funeral.

Practising landing drills in Trebuki bay. About a mile off the beaches, troops transferred to ships'
cutters from warships (if they were in the covering force which had to secure the beaches) or from
transports bringing them from Lemnos. Picket-boats or trawlers towed the cutters in groups
towards the shore and when they could go no further, rowers in the cutters took over. While their
troops rehearsed, RND commanders were taken on naval reconnaissances of the Peninsula. They
briefed their men on the operational plan around 20 April.

Gallipoli began as a naval campaign in which the army had a minor part. But even when the emphasis shifted to the land battle, the navy still had a prominent role. The naval presence guaranteed the resupply of the MEF and its casualty evacuation, while naval gunfire helped to offset the MEF's lack of artillery. Most of the battleships in the naval force were pre-dreadnought designs made obsolete by vessels like HMS *Queen Elizabeth* (above), the Royal Navy's newest battleship and the most powerful afloat. Even though strict limits were placed on her employment, the decision that she should carry out her final gunnery and calibration trials on the Dardanelles forts was a tremendous material and psychological boost for the Gallipoli enterprise.

HMS *Queen Elizabeth* was the first battleship in the world to mount 15-inch guns. Their mighty shells greatly alarmed the Turks when the *QE* bombarded the Narrows forts, firing across the Peninsula from Gaba Tepe on 5 March. But the forts themselves were largely undamaged, while the mobile howitzer batteries around them had already proven almost impossible to detect. As long as these defences held, the minefields keeping the fleet out of the Narrows could not be swept. Turkish morale quickly recovered from the depths to which it had plunged after the loss of the poorly armed Outer Forts on the tip of the Peninsula at the end of February.

HMS *Implacable* with HMS *Queen Elizabeth* (right). This comparison shows to good effect the
modern design of the *QE*. Her graceful lines and the layout of her main armament were duplicated
on most subsequent classes of British battleship.

The battleship HMS *Inflexible*, with the submarine *E7* (far right) at Mudros. The exploits of British submarines during the campaign are legendary. Despite hazardous currents and improving Turkish defences, they penetrated as far as Constantinople itself and at one stage reduced the city to near panic. From May onwards, they practically strangled the Turkish sea lines of communication to the Peninsula. *E7* numbered among the heavy submarine losses. She was caught trying to negotiate the anti-submarine net which the Turks had strung across the Narrows in late July and forced to surrender. HMS *Inflexible* was seriously damaged by shore batteries and a mine during the naval attack on the Narrows on 18 March, and was eventually towed to Malta for repairs. The RND had demonstrated off the western coast of the Peninsula on 18 March, seeking to divert Turkish attention from the Narrows attack.

A *Raglan* class monitor. The arrival off the Peninsula in July of four of these vessels, *Abercrombie*, *Havelock*, *Lord Raglan* and *Lord Roberts*, all mounting twin 14-inch guns, compensated for the loss of heavy naval gunfire support when the battleships were withdrawn after the sinking of *Majestic* and *Triumph* in May. Originally built to bombard the Baltic ports, the monitors were fitted with bulges to give them a shallow draught. While they were thus able to get close to shore, their slow speed and poor manoeuvrability seriously handicapped them in the swift currents of the Dardanelles. The monitors often needed the help of tugs to operate.

The light cruiser HMS *Wymouth*. This photograph is among the first of a British warship in naval camouflage. Warships were rarely painted in disruptive patterns at this time.

43

The dummy HMS *Tiger*. She was one of two merchantmen disguised as battle-cruisers to deceive the Germans into thinking that the Admiralty had denuded the Home Fleet to reinforce the Dardanelles. Even experienced Royal Navy officers were taken in. So was the commander of *U21*, who sank the *Tiger* after his earlier successes against the battleships *Majestic* and *Triumph*. He was astonished to see its wooden superstructure and turrets float away as the ship went under. The other dummy merchantman was deliberately sunk to form a breakwater off Imbros.

The balloon-ship *Hector* raising her kite balloon. *Hector* arrived off the Peninsula in July but the other balloon-ship, the ex-manure carrier *Manica*, had joined the fleet before the landings. As spotters for the fleet, these ships were invaluable because their balloons could stay up all day and their observers could quickly correct the warships' fire by using the telephone the balloons carried. Good spotting on 27 April enabled HMS *Queen Elizabeth* off Gaba Tepe to sink a Turkish ship in the Narrows. The kite balloons could not be used in heavy winds, however, and the balloon-ships had either to move slowly or remain stationary when the balloon was aloft, thus making them vulnerable to submarine attack.

A destroyer bombarding Bulair on the morning of 25 April. Because he considered the narrow Bulair isthmus to be critical for the defence of the Dardanelles, von Sanders concentrated two Turkish divisions in the area. British naval reconnaissance plainly revealed the Turks' feverish efforts to fortify Bulair, which further ruled out a landing there. Hoping to tie down the Turkish garrison instead, Hamilton planned a feint, which the RND successfully carried out. Von Sanders's attention was riveted on the isthmus throughout the first day.

Dawn off Cape Helles. The warship is HMS *Implacable*. The feature on the skyline at centre right is the summit of Achi Baba. This picture shows how Achi Baba could dominate every exit from the Helles beaches, as well as the barrier its wide shoulders formed against any northerly advance up the Peninsula.

Late afternoon, Cape Helles, probably taken around 29 April when the 3rd Field Ambulance
Bearer Division went ashore at W Beach. The glassy water, the darkening sky and the slender
ribbon of coastline combine to create a tranquil setting far removed from the carnage ashore, where
the First Battle of Krithia had just ended. The beauty and strange serenity of the Peninsula, even
during the most bitter fighting, were paradoxes which struck many who served in the Dardanelles.
Few men tired of watching the magnificent sunsets.

A warship bombarding the shore, possibly during one of the Krithia attacks. Note the clear skies and calm sea, which characterize most of the photographs taken in the May-June period. The Aegean coast of the Peninsula lacked sheltered landing places, so the good weather was a godsend to an army which had to be supplied across exposed beaches.

49

The waters off Helles in early May. The sight of hundreds of ships anchored off the coast
heartened the army's spirits, which had been severely battered by events at the landing and by the
First and Second Battles of Krithia. But reports of a U-boat in the Aegean, followed by the
battleship sinkings, quickly transformed this scene. The larger transports were sent to Mudros and
the battleships to Imbros. Men looked at the unfamiliarly barren sea and felt abandoned.

The 1/6th Gurkhas of the 29th Indian Brigade arriving off Helles, perhaps in one of the transports seen in the previous photograph. They distinguished themselves on 12–13 May by capturing bloodlessly what became known as Gurkha Bluff, a Turkish post which had held up all attempts to advance along Gully Spur. During the epic battle of Sari Bair in August, the 1/6th seized and held the important height called Hill Q, before misdirected naval gunfire blasted them off.

HMS *Queen Elizabeth* shelling Turkish positions at Helles. The Turks greatly feared naval gunfire but learned to vacate their trenches and return when the bombardment ended. The effect of the shelling was invariably reduced further because the ships tended to stand too far out to sea, making targets difficult to identify. Poor liaison between the army and the fleet worsened the problems. In one instance on 27 April, one and a half hours elapsed before the ships began firing on an area where a large body of Turks had been reported to be advancing.

A 9.4 inch Krupp gun wrecked in its emplacement at Fort No. 1 on the cliffs of Cape Helles. It was one of nineteen guns in the four forts, two at Helles and two on the Asiatic shore, that comprised the Outer Defences of the Dardanelles. The solid earthwork in front offered ample protection against naval shells with their flat trajectories. So this gun was probably one of several which marine landing parties destroyed on 26 February. The new owners are very much at home, judging by the washing on the improvised clothes line.

Part of the remains of Sedd-el-Bahr village which, together with the medieval fort sheltering it, overlooked the eastern end of V Beach. The fleet pounded the village and the fort as a necessary preliminary to the naval attempt on the Narrows, and again at the landing. But the ruins of the village and the battered walls of the fort gave admirable cover to the Turkish rifleman looking down on V Beach.

Achi Baba from Sedd-el-Bahr village. Although the Helles plan called for the seizure of Achi Baba by the end of the first day, the attackers did not dislodge the Turks from the village until the afternoon of the second day, and then only after severe fighting. Achi Baba was still in Turkish hands at the end of the campaign, nearly nine months later. It takes approximately seven minutes to drive this distance today.

V Beach taken from the Helles cliffs in the vicinity of Fort No. 1. From here and from Sedd-el-Bahr (top left), the Turks had superb enfilade fields of fire across the beach. A heavy barbed wire fence ran along the beach about twenty yards from the water, with a second fence further up the slope behind it. During the V Beach landing, one group of tows, filled with dead and dying Dublin Fusiliers, drifted in the area of the first cluster of piers at the Fort No. 1 end of the beach. Survivors from the *River Clyde* gathered between the second group of piers and the floating pier to the collier. The bank, which runs along the beach immediately behind the strip of sand, is highest there. It marked the limit of the day's advance. On 25 April the sea was coloured crimson well beyond the point where the *River Clyde* had grounded.

V Beach in May, by which time it formed part of the French sector. The French extended the
right flank of the Allied line from the RND trenches across to Morto Bay, which lies on the other
side of Sedd-el-Bahr. The fort eventually became an ammunition depot. Asiatic Annie fired from
the distant coastline.

The *River Clyde* on V Beach in November. The sally-ports cut in her sides, from which she disgorged her infantry, have been covered over and shell fire has badly holed her bows. After the landing, her holds became temporary dressing stations for the wounded. *River Clyde* was refloated in 1919 and sold to a Spanish company, remaining in service until 1966 when she went to the breaker's yard as the *Maruja y Aurora*.

Sedd-el-Bahr from the *River Clyde*. As the collier grounded, a steam hopper was supposed to beach itself in front of her to provide a bridge ashore. But the hopper was swept away. Under the shadow of Sedd-el-Bahr, Commander Unwin, the 51-year-old skipper of the *Clyde*, lashed together two lighters and, with bullets hissing around him, hauled them ashore, where he remained holding the lighters in position as the disembarkation began. After an hour in the water, Unwin collapsed from cold and exhaustion but subsequently returned to help the wounded. Unwin and five others engaged in similar tasks, including Sub-Lieutenant Tisdall of the Anson Battalion, RND, were awarded the Victoria Cross. Amazingly, only one of them was killed. The French built the stone pier when they took over V Beach. Traces of it are still visible.

The Turkish view from Sedd-el-Bahr. The Turkish fire at the landing was particularly intense in the area of the bend in the stone pier, then just a small rocky spit jutting out from the shore. The landing was saved from complete disaster by the return fire from a battery of RND machine guns mounted on the bows of the *River Clyde*, which were commanded by Josiah Wedgewood, the Liberal MP. The lack of ships, the breakwaters and the well-established organization on the beach all suggest that this picture was taken late in the campaign, probably in November. The shell bursting offshore (middle of photograph) testifies to the insecurity of the rear areas at Gallipoli. The men on the beach and the pier seem quite unconcerned.

V Beach, seen here from the *River Clyde*, became a storehouse for the French. The constant activity on both V and W Beaches, particularly at night, created an impression of perpetual motion. Possibly reflecting the different national temperaments, the atmosphere on V was always more lively than on W, its British counterpart.

The hulk of the French battleship *Massena* off V Beach. Built in 1898 and displacing 11 900 tons, she was towed from Toulon and scuttled next to the *River Clyde* on 9 November 1915, to form part of an artificial harbour. Other blockships were also sunk off V and W Beaches for this purpose. They provided valuable shelter to the beaches in the stormy weather before the evacuation.

Part of a rudimentary medical facility on W Beach early in May. The problems it would have had coping with a heavy influx of wounded are self-evident. Note the floating piers improvised from lighters and ships' boats. The battleships *Swiftsure* and *Implacable* lie offshore. Is the chaplain complaining to the medical staff about the conditions or about the careless stacking of the sandbags, which would have reduced the protection they offered against shellfire?

A wounded officer is lowered gently onto a launch from a hospital ship, probably in Malta after his evacuation from W Beach. Largely because GHQ grossly underestimated the likely number of wounded, the casualty evacuation plan collapsed hopelessly in the first weeks of the campaign and struggled to recover thereafter. This picture belies the reality of boatloads of wounded searching vainly for accommodation on filthy transports which were unable to cope with the volume of casualties already aboard. The plight of the wounded was one of the scandals of the campaign and the lurid reports reaching London ensured that the Dardanelles Royal Commission specifically addressed the question when it met in 1917.

Towards the western end of W Beach in May. W was heavily defended by trip wires in the water, barbed wire and mines on the beach, trenches on the slopes overlooking the beach and machine guns hidden in the cliffs enclosing it. But the Lancashire Fusiliers pressed their attack through the wire and up the dunes beyond. In taking W, they lost almost two-thirds of their number. Because collective gallantry hid individual acts of heroism, the Fusiliers were allocated six Victoria Crosses and ordered to choose the recipients. W Beach was renamed Lancashire Landing.

A rare sight at Helles. Timber sleepers, probably for the light railway, and dugouts roofed with corrugated iron, on W Beach. Both timber and corrugated iron were extremely scarce. Telephone wires hang from the three poles on the centre skyline. A fatigue party is extending the terrace at top left.

Dugout accommodation, largely consisting of sandbags piled on terraces and covered over with waterproofs, probably on W Beach. Men lived for months in these conditions, with only brief respites on Lemnos or Mudros, neither of which had the facilities available to troops on leave from the Western Front. Because the beach-head was so small, space was at a premium, particularly in those areas sheltered from direct fire. So the men had to live alongside shells and ammunition boxes stacked snugly against the cliff face. Both the terraces on the cliff, and the road below it, had to be dug out, which helps explain why digging was the most common task for fatigue parties.

Troops from the Second Australian and the New Zealand Infantry Brigades on W Beach, about to embark for Anzac after participating in the Second Battle of Krithia. RND detachments, mainly from the Anson Battalion, took part in the capture of W Beach before reverting to the beach working party duties originally intended for them. The RND HQ landed at W on 29 April. Hunter-Weston's HQ was on the heights above the beach. Proper jetties had been built by the time of the evacuation. Note the ambulance wagons congregated around the hospital on the left.

The coastal road near W Beach about the time of the evacuation. The cliffs are to the west of W.
On 25 April, a group of Fusiliers got ashore unhindered in this vicinity because the cliffs sheltered
them from Turkish fire. They promptly scrambled to the top and took the defences on this flank
in rear, greatly assisting their colleagues in the main frontal assault on W Beach.

Routine traffic in Gully Ravine, close to where it debouched into the sea at Gully Beach, midway between X and Y Beaches. Gully Ravine, running parallel to the western coast, is the widest and deepest of the nullahs which divided the Helles battlefield into three roughly equal sectors. The British held the southern end of Gully Ravine, the Turks the northern. Note the temporary cemetery, touchingly bordered with stones, at bottom right. The carts, moving so freely when this picture was taken, would be bogged down to their axles in December, when bad weather turned the gully floor into a slimy marsh.

A medical detachment secreted in an alcove in Gully Ravine. The rugged beauty of the ravine was striking. Scrub and heather grew wherever they could take root and the shady crevices were alive with flowers. Smaller tributary ravines intersected the main gully at crazy angles. Medical facilities (as shown in the photograph), kitchens, transport, water-carts, animals and dugouts were crammed into them.

Horses picketed in Gully Ravine. The tortuous course of the ravine is readily apparent. Note
the unfinished shelters dug into the cliff face at top right and the man relieving himself
in the bushes above them.

Graffiti decorating the outside walls of dugouts on the heights of Gully Ravine. The interior of the aptly named Grotto, with its expertly chiselled entrance, would have been one of the safest places at Helles, but rather stifling in summer.

British barbed wire entanglements in Gully Ravine. The previous photographs illustrate the importance of Gully Ravine for the British. For the Turks it was vital too. Gully Ravine offered them a secure line of communication up which they could move undetected, and so free from bombardment, to the forward trenches. Consequently the fighting around Gully Ravine was brutal, particularly since Gully Spur, between the defile and the sea, was devoid of cover. On 28 June, a half-mile advance on the spur to Fusilier Bluff cost the British 4000 men; the Turks lost 16 000 in futile counter-attacks over the next week. Gully Ravine and Spur are thick with bones, even now.

Surgeon Taylor outside his dugout in Orchard Gully. He looks fresher and more sprightly in this
picture, which was probably taken in June or July, than he does in the frontispiece photograph.
Taylor would have 'requested leave' to grow his beard. Allowing beards was one way of preserving
naval tradition, thereby ensuring the RND's uniqueness in the British Army. Thus RND soldiers
were referred to as 'ratings' and they probably called Taylor's field ambulance 'the sick bay'.

Dugouts belonging to the officers of the 3rd Field Ambulance above Orchard Gully. An infantryman would have winced at the wasteful way in which scarce corrugated iron has been used to roof the dugouts. Without several layers of sandbags on top, the iron offers only minimal protection. A near miss would have blown these roofs off and stoved in the walls. Perhaps the occupants thought that they were protected sufficiently by the hillside, which rises about 100 feet above the floor of Orchard Gully, and the other ranks' camp, out of picture to the right.

The view from the officers' dugouts towards Achi Baba. The ruins of the Roman aquaduct, which once supplied water to Sedd-el-Bahr, rise above the road to Krithia on centre right. Shrapnel shells are bursting in the air above the front line, indicating that an attack may be underway. The explosions would pepper the infantry beneath with thousands of shrapnel balls. The openness of the battlefield explains why the casualties from the daylight frontal assaults, which were the norm at Helles, were so heavy. The proximity of the 3rd Field Ambulance camp, of which the officers' accommodation formed part, to the trenches is striking.

Looking down from the officers' accommodation onto the 3rd Field Ambulance's camp in Orchard
Gully. Achi Baba is on the left skyline. Apart from the trees and the stunted shrubs, the Krithia
plain is bare, indicating that this picture was taken in June or early July. In the morning little wisps
of smoke from numerous cooking fires would hang in the still air, itself redolent with the smell of
frying bacon. In the evening, the Krithia road, in the left centre, came alive with the rumbling of
men and wagons trekking to and from the trenches. Further on, the light from starshells turned
night into day and cast grotesque shadows in no man's land.

Infantry making their way to the rear through the 3rd Field Ambulance's camp after leaving the line. As a rule, the Turks left alone medical facilities marked by the red cross. But the red cross could not guarantee immunity from shelling when the beach-head was so cramped. And the column on the road constitutes a legitimate target. In that case these flimsy dugouts would offer even less protection than those of the officers. Many are little more than a hole in the ground covered by a waterproof.

Another shot of the 3rd Field Ambulance's dugouts in Orchard Gully. The sun has parched the unshaded ground and a film of dust hangs in the air. The crude shelter on the right might at least catch a cooling breeze but the dugouts were like ovens. To add to their discomforts, the occupants had to share their troglodytic existence with the Peninsula's rich variety of tarantulas, scorpions, giant centipedes and lesser creatures such as ants and beetles. The officers' dugouts are on the ridge to the right.

A staged photograph of the interior of the 3rd Field Ambulance's dressing station in Orchard Gully in summer. Wounded would be brought here by the bearer division. The scenes when a surge of wounded deluged such a facility—as on 14 July when the 2nd Field Ambulance attended to 2000 casualties—do not bear thinking about.

French *poilus* in bivouac near Sedd-el-Bahr. Unlike the British soldier, who was still a volunteer at this time, most of these French troops were conscripts. Wearing red and light blue uniforms and sometimes white cork hats, and advancing accompanied by martial music from bugle and drum, the French lost heavily in the first two battles of Krithia. The intervening Turkish counter-attack almost pushed them into the sea and two RND battalions were sent to reinforce their line. But the French enjoyed some pleasurable compensations. Their red wine was prized by the British. And Asiatic Annie regularly unearthed ancient relics in their sector which inspired a bout of archaeological fever among the *poilus*. Morto Bay is just visible on the right of the picture.

A French 155mm howitzer battery near Sedd-el-Bahr. The shortage of howitzers at Helles made these guns invaluable. Their availability governed the timing of the British attack along Gully Spur at the end of June. The smaller French 75mm batteries also won praise for the accuracy and rapidity of their fire. Their heavy supporting barrage greatly assisted the RND during the Third Battle of Krithia. The large quantities of artillery ammunition which began to arrive regularly from France in June made these concentrated bombardments possible. The French were the envy of the British, who suffered constant ammunition shortages.

A candid shot of the Commander-in-Chief, General Sir Ian Hamilton. His high-collared uniform must have been uncomfortable to wear in the stifling heat. Still, he does look elegant.

An RND signals detachment laying telephone wire. Flying shrapnel frequently cut telephone wires
if they were suspended aerially as seen in many of the photographs. The consequent loss of
communications could be serious, particularly if it happened during a battle. Burying the line,
though much more time-consuming, gave greater protection. And lines to command posts were
laid in duplicate or even triplicate, if the supply of cable allowed.

A RND display in Orchard Gully of some of the weapons used in trench warfare on the Peninsula.
Lt. James, RMLI, is demonstrating a rifle grenade, while in the foreground are various trench
mortars and a hand grenade. Because the War Office did not expect the onset of trench warfare,
the MEF lacked sufficient quantities of the weapons which were essential for trench fighting. It had
to improvise substitutes, such as the catapult and the periscope rifle shown in the centre. Note the
release ratchet on the underside of the catapult and the ill-fitting uniform worn by the
soldier on the right.

A catapult is readied for firing. The photograph shows clearly the wire and canvas basket which
contained the bomb and the lengths of rubber which hurled it. After lighting the fuse on the
bomb, the soldier had seven seconds to fire the catapult by striking the release ratchet underneath,
usually with an entrenching tool. He had to judge the moment carefully, otherwise the bomb
might explode in the air before reaching its target. Range estimates varied between 90 and 200
yards, which testifies to the great inaccuracy of the weapon.

A soldier in an observation post peers through a telescope. He is either watching a specific section of the Turkish line or correcting the fall of shot of artillery or machine guns so that targets are hit. He would pass this information to the appropriate headquarters using the telephone in front of him. The telescope rests on a wooden support and would barely protrude through the protective layers of sandbags. Perhaps an iron loophole, wedged into the sandbags but hidden by the rock ledge, gives added protection against Turkish snipers. They were deadly and could quickly detect the slightest change in the section of trench allotted to them to cover. In this case the sun glinting on the shiny barrel of the telescope, which the soldier has foolishly left uncovered, might attract their attention.

88

An RND machine-gun post. The gun is a Vickers, fed by a belt from the ammunition box near the gunner's right shoulder. He would depress the button between the handgrips to fire it. The telephone enabled him to respond quickly to information passed from observers further forward. In the meantime, the gun would be kept on 'fixed lines', that is, sighted to fire on a target in or behind the Turkish lines. The covering draped over it provides shade and camouflage. The gunner's head so close to the parapet, and the mounting of the gun above it, suggest that this post was located in a support trench, with the gun firing over the heads of the infantry in front. Machine-guns were as deadly on Gallipoli as on the Western Front. The Turk's skilful handling of them came as a nasty shock to the MEF.

A *poilu* sentry using a trench periscope. Sentries would spend their entire watch looking through these devices at the Turkish line opposite. On the *poilu's* left is a periscope rifle, which enabled the firer to aim and shoot without raising his head above the parapet. It was deadly accurate up to 300 yards. The use of sandbags to build up the parapet was a French practice. This photograph was probably taken in December, before the RND had completed its relief of the French above Morto Bay.

90

Officers from the 3rd Field Ambulance watching the flight of a catapult bomb during a visit to Plymouth Avenue. They are holding their periscopes dangerously high. Only the absolute minimum necessary for observation normally protruded above the parapet because Turkish snipers shot out the periscopes as soon as they saw them. An RND officer has taken a break from his magazine to watch the firing but the men seem more interested in the camera.

Reading a newspaper in a trench in the Plymouth Avenue area. Simple holes burrowed into the side of the trench for shelter against the weather represent the most basic form of dugout. The rifles stand in slots cut into the trench wall. Constant pounding from heavy boots has compacted the trench floor, which would be swept clean several times daily to prevent maggots gathering. Sometimes a heaving sea of the revolting creatures entirely obscured the bottom of the trench.

92

A pensive Surgeon Taylor, on the left closest to camera, near Plymouth Avenue. Rifles rest on the parapet ready for firing. This photograph conveys admirably the claustrophobia of the trenches and the enervating heat of summer on the Peninsula.

Standing-to at Fusilier Bluff, probably in October. The firestep and parapet have been built
up with sandbags because digging on this rocky outcrop, overlooking the sea, was so difficult.
The untidiness contrasts with the order of Plymouth Avenue.

A near-miss jolts the camera, blurring the picture. Men can be seen sheltering in the trench on the right.

No. 3 Squadron, Royal Naval Air Service, on its airfield on Tenedos island, twenty miles from Helles. The squadron was led by Commander C.R. Samson, who, in the Portland Naval Review of 1912, became the first pilot to fly an aeroplane off a ship already underway. Samson was easily the best-known airman on the Peninsula. He had established a rough strip at Helles but constant Turkish shelling restricted operations. Only two aircraft were based there during the day, returning to Tenedos at night. From 29 June, even this limited use of Helles airfield became too dangerous and it served for emergency landings only. The aircraft in the picture are Maurice Farman MF11 *Shorthorns*, a French design used by the British (and the Belgians, Italians and Russians). It could carry up to 288lbs of bombs and was the mainstay of Allied land-based aircraft operations in the Dardanelles. A French squadron, No. 98T, also flew from Tenedos. It was much better equipped regarding personnel, spare parts, transport, workshops and hangars, than the British squadron.

HMS *Ark Royal*, probably in Kephalo Bay, Imbros. Originally designed as a tramp steamer, she was the Royal Navy's first seaplane carrier and had been active in the Dardanelles since late February 1915. *Ark Royal* could carry up to ten aircraft, which the steam-driven hoists winched from their hangar in the hold. Two German aircraft bombed her on 25 March. The first bomb missed by 100 yards, the second by only ten. Another carrier, HMS *Ben My Chree* arrived on 12 July, having formerly been a Liverpool–Isle of Man passenger ferry.

This photograph, and the three following, depict HMS *Ark Royal* winching aboard one of her Short Seaplanes. The Short Seaplane, Admiralty Type 827, had a maximum speed of 61 mph and a ceiling of about 2000 feet. Small bombs were suspended from a tray under the fuselage and folding wings facilitated stowage on warships. The Short 184, a later type carried on HMS *Ben My Chree*, carried out the first successful aerial torpedo attack in history, when it torpedoed a large Turkish transport off Bulair on 12 August 1915.

Among the principal tasks of aircraft were reconnaissance and spotting, for which the *Ark Royal's* seaplanes were fitted with wireless telegraphy (unlike the land-based aircraft, which did not have wireless installed until later in the campaign). But the wireless equipment was unreliable, no modern cameras were available, the maps were inaccurate and insufficiently detailed, and the observers lacked proper training. Even when information was gained, it was often poorly used. Thus beaches that pilots reported as well-defended turned out to be those selected for the landings on 25 April. Reconnaissance at Suvla showed that the British faced no serious opposition for two days after their landing on 6–7 August but they did not advance.

The seaplanes also flew as bombers, dropping flechettes (metal-winged darts) and small bombs. The engineers and armourers on HMS *Ark Royal* rigged up a system for releasing the bombs by pulling a wire, which proved very successful. It was a boost for Samson's squadron, in particular, which ranged all over the Peninsula, bombing camps, supply bases and columns of marching troops. Whereas the effect of German aircraft on the MEF was minimal, the Turks greatly feared the British airmen.

100

Although the Short Seaplane was armed with a machine-gun in the observer's cockpit for self-defence, aerial combat on the Peninsula was rare. But Turkish anti-aircraft fire, though ineffective in the beginning, gradually improved, and had brought down six aircraft when the campaign ended.

A Sopwith *Schneider* suspended alongside the Short Seaplane on HMS *Ark Royal*. A seaplane development of the successful Sopwith *Tabloid*, the *Schneider* won the 1912 Schneider Trophy race at Monaco and afterwards attained a speed of 42 mph, then a record for a seaplane. The Admiralty ordered twelve, with modifications such as a machine-gun mounting on the top wing. Ultimately 136 were produced. The *Schneider's* performance deteriorated as more equipment was added to it. Sometimes it was unable to take off even in the calm Dardanelles seas.

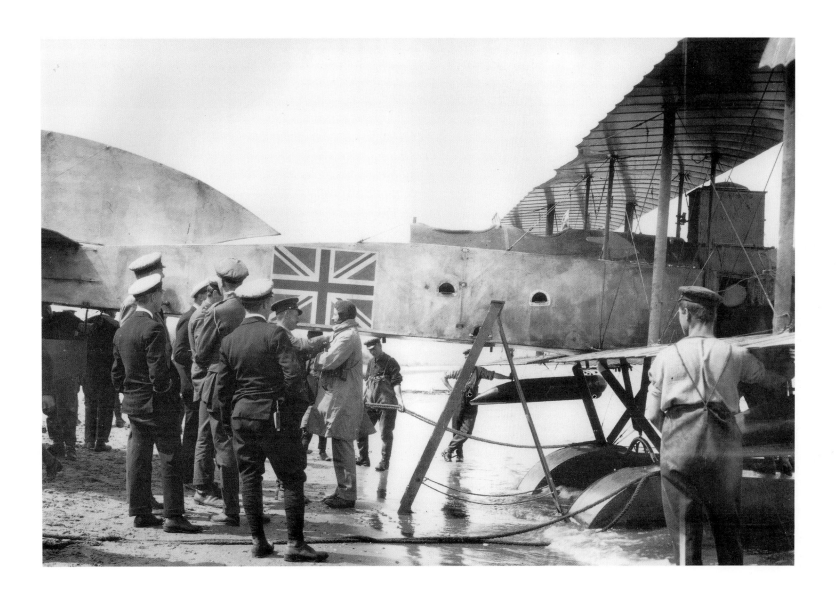

Captain Kilner, a prominent Royal Marine Pilot in the Dardanelles, adjusts an observer's equipment before a Short Seaplane takes off on a sortie. Many of these lumbering seaplanes had trouble getting above 2000 feet and so flew within range of Turkish small-arms fire. On 4 March, one collected 28 bullet holes. As well as this danger, the seaplane crews had to contend with the disgusting stench of the trenches, which could be smelt as high as 4000 feet. The weather-beaten appearance of the above aircraft suggests that this photograph (and the next one), were probably taken in the Gulf of Stavros, after the campaign.

The seaplane crews often felt that they were the poor cousins of the Dardanelles air war because of the attention lavished on Samson. He invariably had at least ten machines on strength and, in July, received six of the latest *Nieuport* scouts. But HMS *Ark Royal* usually had only its six ancient seaplanes, which were almost irreplaceable as spares took so long to arrive from England. The crews also thought that the fixation with land-based aircraft led to the neglect of the seaplane's potential. Had the advance proceeded steadily up the Peninsula as planned, the MEF would have relied heavily on seaplanes because of the lack of aerodromes from which the land-based types could operate.

Though the shortage of water at Helles was never so acute as at Anzac or Suvla, a wash such as these two officers are enjoying in Orchard Gully was nonetheless a luxury. A senior German officer attached to the Turks commented that their limitless supplies of fresh water underpinned much of the Turks' tenacity. Had they been subjected to the thirst which constantly afflicted the MEF, their performance would have fallen off badly. Note the down-at-heel sneakers worn by the officer on the left, an example of how the trying conditions on the Peninsula quickly broke down the conservative standards of a peace-time British officers' mess.

Tonsorial treatment in Orchard Gully. Close cropped hair was cooler and less likely to attract lice. The Peninsula strain was particularly virulent and appeared to thrive on Keating's powder, which the army issued to eradicate the pests. Few men escaped their attentions. Thus the uniform of the soldier above was probably lousy. Whenever he could, he would turn it inside out and run a burning cigarette end up the seams. The cracking sound of frying lice was music to the ears of the troops they tormented.

A field kitchen at Helles, probably in June or July. As soon as the lids were lifted off the cooking pots, the contents would disappear beneath a sea of blue-green 'corpse' flies. The pest reached plague levels in the unsanitary conditions and was largely responsible for the dysentery which enfeebled the MEF in the summer months. Empty ration boxes are used as firewood.

A bakery on Imbros. It may have sent some bread to Helles, but until mobile bakeries were set up there, British and Dominion troops largely went without fresh bread. Typically, the French had it almost from the outset.

Officers dining at the 3rd Field Ambulance Officers' Mess. The table and chairs are made from old biscuit and instrument boxes, while the open tins and dixies are a far cry from the mess silver. Still, the two soldiers on the left, acting as stewards, ensure that some semblance of an officers' mess service is provided. But unless these officers were able to purloin delicacies from a hospital ship, they faced the same monotonous diet of bully, bacon, and apricot or plum jam, all turned liquid by the heat, which many men found so revolting. Fresh fruit and vegetables were almost unknown and fresh meat, also a rarity, was quickly turned rancid by the flies.

Two soldiers modelling primitive respirators at Helles. The one on the right is the black-veil type, the one on the left a P Helmet Mark 1, which the soldier should have tucked into his shirt. Apart from a few tear-gas grenades thrown at Anzac, gas was not used on the Peninsula but gas drills were occasionally practised. These soldiers were more likely to be seeking a respite from the flies, which tended to assault the eyes, nose and mouth—or anywhere else where moisture collected.

Men—and horses—frolicking in the sea. A splash in the Aegean offered an escape from the tedium and misery of life on the Peninsula. Its uplifting effect more than offset the risk from Turkish shelling. And in practical terms, it was the only chance men had to get a decent wash. But the Director of Medical Services, Surgeon-General Birrell, did not number among the advocates of sea bathing. He thought that it could be responsible for the dysentery epidemic.

Four of the 1255 Greek labourers employed at Helles at the end of October. They are helping to build winter dugouts on Officers' Walk above X Beach. An Egyptian and a Maltese Labour Corps worked at Anzac and a mixed group of 800 civilians at Suvla. The use of civilian labourers obviated the need to draw on men who could ill be spared from the trenches and whose poor health would have deteriorated further if they had to do the heavy fatigue tasks the labourers undertook. But most of these civilian workers were of little use if employed under shellfire.

The Officers' Walk dugouts overlooked Implacable Landing, as X Beach was otherwise known. While supporting the landing at X on 25 April, HMS *Implacable* came so close to the beach to bombard the Turks that she almost grounded. They were too stunned by her fire to offer much resistance to the Royal Fusiliers coming ashore but the Fusiliers lost heavily trying to link up with W Beach to the south. Disciplinary action against *Implacable's* captain, for continuing to fire when the boats had reached the shore, was dropped once her contribution to the success of the landing was recognized. Note the gutter for water runoff in the centre of the picture.

Completed dugouts on Officers' Walk in November. The 2nd and 3rd Field Ambulances had now amalgamated, forming the X Beach Field Ambulance. Note the box frames used as windows and the brick chimney. The path in front led down to lower levels and eventually to the beach. One hopes that none of the occupants of Officers' Walk were sleepwalkers. When the RND took over part of the French sector in December, it found that dugouts of this standard were commonplace there.

A southerly look along Officers' Walk. The photographs on pp. 112 and 113 show how sturdily these dugouts were built and how materials hitherto rarely available on the Peninsula were extensively used in their construction. As much hutting timber as was on hand in England and Egypt, and some 5000 tons of corrugated iron, were ordered for the Dardanelles at this time. The need for protection both from winter, and from the heavy guns which the Germans were expected to send to Gallipoli, prompted this investment. But even as these dugouts were taking shape, the evacuation of the Peninsula had already been decided upon in principle in London.

This photograph, and the two following, depict the interiors of dugouts on Officers' Walk. Personal touches, and improvisation, which in some cases is ingenious, have ensured a high standard of comfort. A pair of slippers lie on the spotless floor beside a bedside table, which was formerly a box for tins of Libby McNeill corned beef. Strips of hessian screen the neatly made bed from the rough stone wall. A candle in a biscuit tin serves as a reading lamp. And a dud Turkish shell stands against the bedstead.

A variation on the same theme. A pipe rack hangs from the wall, above the dazzling quilt on the bed. The flue from the home-made stove has been cemented into the wall. The marmalade box serves as a container for firewood. Other boxes double up as shelving for books and knick-knacks.

Muslin curtains soften the light as it falls on the prominently displayed photograph of loved ones.
A battered walking stick (what British officer didn't carry one) leans against the wall. Letters
from home are kept on the third shelf on the right. They would have been
read—and reread—many times.

118

A homely scene in the X Beach Ambulance Officers' Mess. Note the enormous fireplace, the immaculate uniforms and the polished boots. Padre Hallding, the RND's Wesleyan chaplain, has forsaken leggings for woolly knee-length socks. The field service table, folding, is still in military use, its design largely unchanged from the example in the photograph.

Officers' Mess celebrations in full swing, possibly for Surgeon Taylor's birthday or for Christmas. The glow on the revellers' faces would have been due to the contents of the well-stocked table rather than the box of Peak Frean's standard biscuits in the background. These biscuits were so hard that men broke their teeth off trying to bite into them. The men were then treated by a 'dentist' who was probably unqualified. One at Anzac had previously been a blacksmith.

Perhaps the most remarkable photograph in the collection. The blur above the headland is a
German aircraft which has just bombed the area south of X Beach. The explosion stands out
clearly against the skyline. Unlike the pilot of this aircraft, the Germans usually flew very high.
Their twenty-pound bombs were ineffectual, inflicting less than twenty casualties
throughout the campaign.

RND officers in a variety of winter ensembles, probably just after the blizzard which struck
Gallipoli in late November. Most of the 16 000 frost-bite cases and 280 deaths were from Suvla,
where the troops were dreadfully exposed on the open plain. Helles did not suffer too badly. Still,
the universal hope there was for a cook's fire that would burn in spite of the weather. A
comparison between this photograph and the beach scene on p. 111 illustrates how drastically
winter transformed the Peninsula.

122

A pile of dummy soldiers ready for use just before the evacuation, one of a number of subterfuges designed to convince the Turks that the strength of the Helles garrison was being kept up. Others included maintaining normal levels of small arms and shell-fire, marching in the rear areas in view of the Turks, and leaving tents erected. On the last night rifles were rigged to fire automatically. The withdrawals from Anzac and Suvla have justly been hailed as military masterpieces. The bloodless evacuation of Helles three weeks later, under the noses of an alerted enemy, perhaps deserves even higher praise.

Loaded with firewood, ambulance wagons from the 2nd Field Ambulance go ashore at Stavros in late February 1916. After the evacuation from Gallipoli, one RND brigade garrisoned both Mudros and Tenedos while the other was sent to Salonika, where it held the right flank of the Allied line on the Gulf of Stavros. The Anglo-French Salonika expedition was intended to deter a Bulgarian sally into northern Greece and to aid Romania if she entered the war on the Allied side. The Germans called Salonika 'their largest internment camp' because half a million Allied troops were idly bottled up there almost until the Armistice.

The 2nd Field Ambulance Camp at Rendina Gorge, Stavros, in March 1916. The neat, precisely laid out, and well-spaced lines contrast starkly with the cramped confusion of the Peninsula. White stones border the flag station and the carefully tended gardens. The paths are spotless.

The bearer division of the 2nd Field Ambulance parading before an exercise at Stavros. Many of these men would have joined the unit shortly before the evacuation or had arrived since as replacements for the losses incurred during the campaign.

The opposing armies were not in contact at Stavros and the RND's duties amounted to improving
the defences in its sector (a favourite pastime for armies with nothing to do) and intercepting
Greek stragglers. The numerous jackals roaming the hills, and the occasional aeroplane, vied with
each other as the main threats facing the RND. The countryside was rugged and largely
uncultivated, with primitive roads and tracks connecting villages whose way of life had not changed
for centuries. In this peaceful and healthy environment, the RND could recuperate from the
enfeebling effects of the campaign.

An officer reflects on the peaceful shore of Lake Besika, Stavros. What lies ahead?
The Western Front? It can't be worse than Gallipoli . . . can it?

A Note on the Provenance of the Collection

Ross Bastiaan

The collection of photographs from which the pictures in this book were selected first came to my attention when I was a graduate periodontal student in London in 1977. Keith Taylor, then photographer at the London Royal Dental Hospital, showed me 600 negatives which he had acquired at the closing-down sale of the London photographic store James A. Sinclair in 1976. They had been lodged at Sinclair's in 1931, when it was customary for negatives to be left with a reputable photographic store so that prints could be made and mailed on request. Indeed, the paper sleeves containing the individual negatives show pencil strokes indicating the number of prints made from that negative. The box containing the negatives had not been touched for many years and lay neglected on a dusty top shelf at Sinclair's before Keith Taylor obtained them.* In 1985, he forwarded the negatives to me in Australia. I approached the Australian War Memorial, who promptly printed them and returned both the negatives and the prints to me.

As well as forming a pictorial record of the Gallipoli campaign, the collection throws light on the nature of war photography in 1915. In some respects, it had changed little since the Boer War. Pictures taken then, sometimes by soldiers, depicted largely static scenes. Actual combat shots were rare — just as they are rare in this collection. Newspapers relied instead on war artists to recreate battle scenes. Censorship regulations, which circumscribed the activities of war photographers, necessitated the continuation of this reliance on war artists at the start of the First World War.

Soldiers taking photographs, however, were largely ignored. To encourage them to take battle-zone pictures, newspapers ran photographic competitions with substantial prizes for the winning entries. In England the Proprietors' Association of Press Photo-

---

* Because the box bore the surname Taylor, and Surgeon Taylor served at Gallipoli, he was most probably the photographer. Surgeon Taylor was not related to Keith Taylor.

graphic Agencies (PAPPA)—including Alfieri's, Central News, Central Press Photos, London News Agency, News Illustrated, Sport & General Press Agency, Topical, Barratts—purchased or paid a commission for these photographs. Unfortunately the majority of them were uncaptioned perhaps for censorship reasons, and except in the case of a few comprehensive collections, such as those of Lieutenant Money, Sergeant Pilkington and Private Fyfe, the actual photographers remained unknown.

Kodak facilitated the wider use of photography in the trenches by manufacturing simple and inexpensive cameras which could be attached to army belts or folded into compact units for carrying in haversacks. Advertisements showed the British soldier carrying his camera to war, and a great amount of literature on photography was available to him. But concern at the rapid expansion in the number of these amateur photographers prompted the British High Command late in 1915 to issue an order restricting the use of cameras to one camera per battalion (800 men). After 1915 the greater importance accorded to Official War Photographers largely satisfied press demands for photographic coverage of

A Kodak No. 1 Junior camera, similar to the one used to take the photographs in this book. Beside the camera is a magnesium ribbon flash unit. The dugout photographs in the book were taken with this simple device.

The popularity of amateur photography for the private soldier is illustrated in this advertisement from *The Australasian Photo-Review* of 15 May 1915.

the battlefield. The military were also satisfied because these official photographers were under their strict control.

The official photographer to the Mediterranean Expeditionary Force was Ernest Brooks, a pre-war professional photographer with the *Daily Mail*. In all, he took 550 photographs, which were forwarded to the Official Press Bureau for censorship. The Bureau, controlled by the Home Office, then released the photographs to Central News for publication, but after other press agencies complained to the Home Office of a monopoly, Brooks's negatives were distributed in rotation to all members of PAPPA. These negatives now form the most significant part of the Imperial War Museum's Gallipoli collection of 1400 photographs.

The advantages of owning a camera were obvious, both for those at home and at the front, as can be seen from this advertisement from *The Australasian Photo-Review* of 15 May 1915.

The paucity of official war photographs in the early years of the war prompted agencies to offer soldiers generous rewards for their photographs.

Surgeon A. G. Crooks also donated his Gallipoli collection of 120 photographs to the Museum. Crooks and the photographer of the works in this book often shot the same scene, sometimes with only a few seconds separating the photographs. The quality of their pictures is outstanding. The same cannot be said of most of the other unofficial photographs taken during the campaign. They amount to little more than snapshots, intended for the photographer's family album.

Most Australian photographs of the campaign belong in this latter category. Because no official photographer accompanied the Anzacs on the Peninsula, the only Australian photographs which could even be remotely described as official were those taken by C. E. W. Bean, the official Australian correspondent (and later, official historian). Rarely venturing from Anzac, he spent only eleven days at Helles, where he recorded mainly the Anzac battles. Bean's negatives, which are in the Australian War Memorial's Gallipoli collection, comprise a large proportion of the few photographs known to have been taken by Australians at Helles.

The photographs of Helles in this book were shot with a 1914 No. 1 Kodak Junior camera, which had a sliding bellows focusing system and a four and a half inch meniscus achromatic lens with a Kodak ball-bearing shutter system. Shutter speeds of 1/25, 1/50 and 1/100 of a second were available. The camera cost US$8, weighed 23 ounces and measured 1 7/16 × 3 5/8 × 6 5/8 inches. The film size was 120, and the negative measured 2¼ by 3¼ inches. The panchromatic roll film was readily available at the time and used in most folding cameras. It was typical of other small cameras of the period, such as the Ensign and Butchers (England) and the Goery (Germany).

Kodak had also added an autographic feature to its existing models in 1914, consisting of a small door on the back of the camera which could be opened to allow the user to write directly onto the film with a special stylus, supplied with the camera. The popular folding cameras of the time were quickly replaced with newer models incorporating this feature. The negatives in this collection show no such markings, and therefore it is unlikely that the photographer had the newer type of camera.

But he would have had a portrait attachment for close-up work. He probably lit a six-inch strip of magnesium ribbon flash for the shots of dugout interiors. It burned with an excellent yellow light for up to six seconds. If, as is likely, the photographer was indeed Surgeon Taylor, he could have used his position as a commanding officer to seek the assistance of the Royal Naval Air Service darkroom on Imbros, which developed negatives taken on aerial reconnaissance sorties, to process his prints. That help detracts little from what he achieved with the primitive equipment at his disposal. These clear, well-resolved and composed photographs are a tribute to him.

Notes

1. The service record of Surgeon C.H.S. Taylor is held by the Defence Medical Services Directorate, Ministry of Defence in London.
2. Much of this paragraph was drawn from G.A. Law, 'The Evolution of the Field Ambulance 1906 to 1918' in *Defence Force Journal*, No. 66, Sept./Oct. 87, pp. 53–7.
3. M. Gilbert, *Winston Spencer Churchill. III. The Challenge of War 1914–1916*, Boston, 1971, p. 48.
4. D. Jerrold, *The Royal Naval Division*, London, 1923.
5. M. Middlebrook (ed.), *The Diaries of Private Horace Bruckshaw, Royal Marine Light Infantry, 1915–16*, London, 1979, p. xx.
6. B.H. Liddell Hart, *History of the First World War*, London, 1970, p. 183.
7. J. North, *Gallipoli, The Fading Vision*, London, 1936, p. 41.
8. L.C.F. Turner, *The First World War*, Melbourne, 1967, p. 16.
9. M.E. Occleshaw, 'The Munitions Myth' in *The Gallipolian*, No. 52, Winter 1986, p. 26.
10. General Sir Ian Hamilton quoted by R. Rhodes James, 'General Sir Ian Hamilton' in Field Marshal Sir Michael Carver (ed.), *The War Lords*, London, 1976, p. 86.
11. Maj.-Gen. E.K.G. Sixsmith, *British Generalship in the Twentieth Century*, London, 1970, p. 62.

12. ibid., p. 148.
13. R. Rhodes James, *Gallipoli*, London, 1974, p. 57.
14. The photograph of Hamilton aboard HMS *Triad* can be seen in A. Moorehead, *Gallipoli*, South Melbourne, 1975, p. 80.
15. P.A. Pedersen, *Monash as Military Commander*, Melbourne, 1985, p. 54.
16. *First Report of the Dardanelles Royal Commission. Part 2. Conduct of Operations*, HMSO, London, 1917, p. 16.
17. C.F. Aspinall-Oglander, *History of the Great War. Military Operations. Gallipoli*, I, London, 1929, p. 119.
18. Bruckshaw, op. cit., p. 19.
19. H.M. Denham, *Dardanelles. A Midshipman's Diary*, London, 1981, p. 50.
20. J. Masefield, *Gallipoli*, Melbourne, 1978, p. 33.
21. J. Murray, *Gallipoli 1915*, London, 1977, p. 60.
22. Aspinall-Oglander, op. cit., I, p. 125.
23. Hunter-Weston in Bruckshaw, op. cit., pp. 26–7.
24. Brooke in Jerrold, op. cit., pp. 66–7.
25. Rhodes James, *Gallipoli*, p. 86.
26. Birrell's memorandum of 18 April is in Maj.-Gen. Sir W.G. McPherson and Maj. T.J. Mitchell, *History of the Great War. Medical Services–General History*, IV, London, 1924, pp. 19–20.
26. E.W. Bush, *Gallipoli*, London, 1975, p. 119.

28. Moorehead, op. cit., p. 99.
29. Air Commodore C.R. Samson in P.H. Liddle, *Men of Gallipoli*, London, 1976, p. 126.
30. Liddell Hart, op. cit., p. 233.
31. Liddle, op. cit., p. 136.
32. Liman von Sanders, *Five Years in Turkey*, Maryland, 1927, pp. 63–5.
33. Murray, op. cit., p. 65.
34. Bruckshaw, op. cit., p. 30.
35. ibid., p. 31.
36. Aspinall-Oglander, op. cit., I, p. 215.
37. Bush, op. cit., p. 150.
38. Rhodes James, *Gallipoli*, p. 137.
39. J. Laffin, *Damn the Dardanelles!*, South Melbourne, 1985, p. 62.
40. Moorehead, op. cit., p. 111.
41. General Sir I. Hamilton, *Gallipoli Diary*, I, London, 1920, p. 176.
42. Rhodes James, *Gallipoli*, pp. 142–3.
43. Murray, op. cit., p. 66.
44. Moorehead, op. cit., p. 147.
45. Murray, op. cit., pp. 68–9.
46. ibid., p. 103.
47. Lt. Savory quoted in Liddle, op. cit., p. 177.
48. Aspinall-Oglander, op. cit., II, p. 48.
49. Churchill in Bush, op. cit., p. 202.
50. Hunter-Weston in Rhodes James, *Gallipoli*, pp. 210, 231.
51. C.S. Forester, *The General*, London, 1979, p. 173.
52. Aspinall-Oglander, op. cit., I, p. 332.
53. Rhodes James, *Gallipoli*, p. 201.
54. North, op. cit., p. 144.

55 Jerrold, op. cit., p. 113.
56 C.E.W. Bean, *Anzacs to Amiens*, Canberra, 1968, p. 124.
57 See for example entry for 2 May 1915, Bean Diary 5; 3 May, Diary 7; 24 May, Diary 8, Bean Collection, Australian War Memorial (AWM). Capt. W.A. Forsythe, diary entry for 4 May 1915, File 8/13, AWM.
58 Maj.-Gen. Sir J. Gellibrand, diary entry for 4 May 1915, Folder 187/38, Gellibrand Collection, AWM.
59 L.J. Bain to N. Wanliss, 17 November 1921, File 8/13, AWM.
60 Birdwood in Rhodes James, *Gallipoli*, p. 70. General Sir John Monash, diary entry for 8 May 1915, Monash Collection, National Library of Australia.
61 Bruckshaw, op. cit., pp. 58–68.
62 D. Winter, *Death's Men*, London, 1979, p. 89.
63 A.P. Herbert, *The Secret Battle*, Oxford, 1982, p. 32.
64 Bruckshaw, op. cit., p. 45.
65 Rhodes James, *Gallipoli*, pp. 156–7.
66 C. Mackenzie, *Gallipoli Memories*, London, 1929, pp. 111–12.
67 Hamilton, op. cit., I, p. 177.
68 Moorehead, op. cit., p. 150.
69 Bruckshaw, op. cit., p. 50.
70 Aspinall-Oglander, op. cit., II, p. 38.
71 Bruckshaw, op. cit., p. 56.
72 Aspinall-Oglander, op. cit., II, p. 99.
73 Moorehead, op. cit., p. 153.
74 Murray, op. cit., pp. 88–9.

75 Fears that the Turks might employ gas were unfounded. But a few tear gas grenades were used at Anzac.
76 Jerrold, op. cit., p. 146.
77 Moorehead, op. cit., p. 157.
78 Field Marshal Sir W.R. Birdwood, *Khaki and Gown*, London, 1941, p. 262.
79 Rhodes James, *Gallipoli*, p. 225. Unlike the French, who quickly adopted Mudros as their main base, a decision which worked well.
80 F.M. Cutlack (ed.), *War Letters of General Monash*, Sydney, 1934, p. 74.
81 Aspinall-Oglander, op. cit., II, p. 73.
82 ibid., pp. 117–18.
83 Hamilton, op. cit., II, p. 8.
84 Murray, op. cit., p. 120.
85 A.G. Butler, *Official History of the Australian Army Medical Services*, I, Melbourne, 1930, p. 240. McPherson and Mitchell, op. cit., IV, p. 59.
86 Rhodes James, *Gallipoli*, p. 222.
87 Gasparich in Liddle, op. cit., p. 245.
88 Bruckshaw, op. cit., p. 86.
89 For the genesis of the August plan, see Pedersen, op. cit., pp. 303–5.
90 A.J. Hill in C.E.W. Bean, *Official History of Australia in the War of 1914–18. II. The Story of Anzac*, St. Lucia, 1981, p. xxix.
91 Rhodes James in *The War Lords*, p. 92.
92 Murray, op. cit., p. 125.
93 Jerrold, op. cit., p. 148.
94 The Collingwood and Benbow Battalions of the First Naval Brigade were

disbanded after the Third Battle of Krithia. See p. 11.
95 Murray, op. cit., pp. 196–7.
96 Jerrold, op. cit., p. 159.
97 Aspinall-Oglander, op. cit., II, pp. 385–6.
98 Murray, op. cit., p. 212.
99 P.H. Liddle, *Gallipoli 1915. Pens, Pencils and Cameras at War*, London, 1985, p. xix.
100 B.H. Liddell Hart, *Through the Fog of War*, London, 1938, p. 295.
101 Murray, op. cit., p. 222.
102 Rhodes James, *Gallipoli*, p. 348.
103 Jerrold, op. cit., p. 169.
104 Liddell Hart, *History of the First World War*, p. 207.
105 Jerrold, op. cit., pp. 169–70.
106 See for example Bruckshaw, op. cit., pp. 101–7.
107 Jerrold, op. cit., p. 338.
108 Aspinall-Oglander, op. cit., I, p. 343.
109 C. Falls, *The Great War*, New York, 1959, p. 135.
110 P.H. Liddle, 'The Distinctive Nature of the Gallipoli Experience', in *Journal of the Royal United Services Institute for Defence Studies*, Vol. 122, No. 2, June 1977, p. 52.
111 North, op. cit., p. 32.
112 For a description of the Peninsula today, see P.A. Pedersen, 'The Ghosts of Anzac', in *Journal of the Australian War Memorial*, No. 2, April 1983, pp. 34–42.
113 Hamilton in Moorehead, op. cit., p. 234.

Select Bibliography

I MANUSCRIPT SOURCES

AUSTRALIAN WAR MEMORIAL, CANBERRA

Bean, C. E. W., Collection, including diaries from the Gallipoli period.
Gellibrand, Maj.-Gen. Sir J., Papers.
Source notes for battalion histories. File 8/13, entitled '14 Bn History'.

NATIONAL LIBRARY OF AUSTRALIA

Monash, Gen. Sir J., Collection.

MINISTRY OF DEFENCE, LONDON.
(Defence Medical Services Directorate)

Taylor, Surgeon C. H. S., Service record.

II OFFICIAL SOURCES

AUSTRALIAN WAR MEMORIAL, CANBERRA

First Report of the Dardanelles Royal Commission. Part 2. Conduct of Operations, HMSO, London, 1917.

III OFFICIAL HISTORIES

AUSTRALIA

Bean, C. E. W., *Official History of Australia in the War of 1914–18. II. The Story of Anzac*, St. Lucia, 1981.
Butler, A. G., *Official History of the Australian Army Medical Services 1914–18*, I, Melbourne, 1930.

UNITED KINGDOM

Corbett, Sir J. S., *History of the Great War. Naval Operations*, III, London, 1923.
Aspinall-Oglander, Brig.-Gen. C. F., *History of the Great War. Military Operations. Gallipoli*, I, London, 1929; II, London, 1932.
McPherson, Maj-Gen. Sir W. G. and Mitchell, Maj. T. J., *History of the Great War, Medical Services—General History*, IV, London, 1924.

IV BOOKS AND ARTICLES

Bean, C. E. W., *Anzac to Amiens*, Canberra, 1968.
Birdwood, Field Marshal Sir W. R., *Khaki and Gown*, London, 1941.
Bush, E. W., *Gallipoli*, London, 1975.
Cutlack, F. M. (ed.), *War Letters of General Monash*, Sydney, 1934.
Denham, H. M., *Dardanelles. A Midshipman's Diary*, London, 1981.
Falls, C., *The Great War*, New York, 1959.
Forester, C. S., *The General*, London, 1979.
Gilbert, M., *Winston Spencer Churchill. III. The Challenge of War 1914–1916*, Boston, 1971.
Hamilton, Gen. Sir I., *Gallipoli Diary*, 2 vols, London, 1920.
Herbert, A. P., *The Secret Battle*, Oxford, 1982.
Jane, F. T. (ed.), *Fighting Ships—1914*, London, 1914.
Jerrold, D., *The Royal Naval Division*, London, 1923.
Laffin, J., *Damn the Dardanelles!*, South Melbourne, 1985.
Law, G. A., 'The Evolution of the Field Ambulance 1906 to 1918', in *Defence Force Journal*, No. 66, Sept./Oct. 87, pp. 53–7.
Liddell Hart, Sir B. H., *History of the First World War*, London, 1970.
——, *Through the Fog of War*, London, 1938.
Liddle, P. H., *Men of Gallipoli*, London, 1976.
——, *Gallipoli, 1915. Pens, Pencils and Cameras at War*, London, 1985.
——, 'The Distinctive Nature of the Gallipoli Experience', in *Journal of the Royal United Services Institute for Defence Studies*, Vol. 122, No. 2, June 1977, pp. 51–6.
Mackenzie, C., *Gallipoli Memories*, London, 1929.
Marder, A. J., *From the Dardanelles to Oran*, London, 1974.
Masefield, J., *Gallipoli*, Melbourne, 1978.
Middlebrook, M. (ed.), *The Diaries of Private Horace Bruckshaw, Royal Marine Light Infantry, 1915–16*, London, 1979.
Moorehead, A., *Gallipoli*, South Melbourne, 1975.
Munson, K., *Aircraft of World War One*, Surrey, 1968.
Murray, J., *Gallipoli 1915*, London, 1977.
North, J., *Gallipoli: The Fading Vision*, London, 1936.
Occleshaw, M. E., 'The Munitions Myth', in *The Gallipolian*, No. 52, Winter 1986, pp. 22–9.

Pedersen, P. A., *Monash as Military Commander*, Melbourne, 1985.
———, 'The Ghosts of Anzac', in *Journal of the Australian War Memorial*, No. 2, April 1983, pp. 34–42.
Rhodes James, R., *Gallipoli*, London, 1974.
———, 'General Sir Ian Hamilton', in Field Marshal Sir Michael Carver (ed.), *The War Lords*, London, 1976, pp. 84–93.
Sixsmith, Maj.-Gen. E. K. G., *British Generalship in the Twentieth Century*, London, 1970.
Taylor, J. W. R. (ed.), *Combat Aircraft of the World*, New York, 1969.
Turner, L. C. F., *The First World War*, Melbourne, 1967.
von Sanders, Marshal Liman, *Five Years in Turkey*, Maryland, 1927.
Winter, D., *Death's Men*, London, 1979.

GREAT BATTLES
OF THE
GREAT WAR

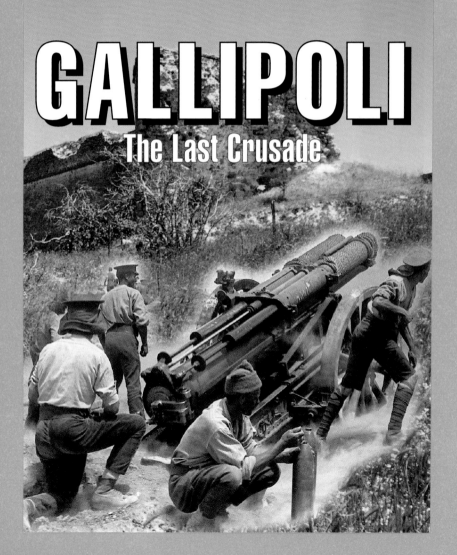

GALLIPOLI
The Last Crusade

This highly acclaimed three part documentary series explores and explains the greatest set-piece battles of the First World War – Gallipoli, the Somme and Ypres. Rare film and photographic archive, together with stunning location filming combine to bring these pivotal battles to the screen in a unique way.

Volume 1 – GALLIPOLI

In April 1915 this was the location for the infamous allied attempt to take the Turkish held Gallipoli Peninsula and control the entrance to the Black Sea. The failed naval attack and subsequent seaborne landings at ANZAC and Cape Helles ended in humiliating retreat and cost over one hundred thousand lives from all sides.